Preparing Candidates
for
CONFIRMATION & BELIEVERS' BAPTISM

✡ ✡ ✡

A HANDBOOK

for
Pastors' & Teachers'

Preparing Candidates
for
CONFIRMATION & BELIEVERS' BAPTISM

✣ ✣ ✣

A HANDBOOK

for

PASTORS' & TEACHERS'

Ernest W. Talibuddin
(The Church of North India)

**ISPCK
2008**

Preparing Candidates for Confirmation & Believers' Baptism - A HANDBOOK for Pastors' & Teachers' — Published by the Rev. Dr. Ashish Amos of the Indian Society for Promoting Christian Knowledge (ISPCK), Post Box 1585, 1654, Madarsa Road, Kashmere Gate, Delhi-110006.

© Ernest W. Talibuddin, 2008

All rights reserved. No part of this book may be reproduced or transmitted in any form or by any means, electronic, mechanical, photocopying, recording, or by any information storage and retrieval system, without the prior permission in writing from the publisher.

The views expressed in the book are those of the author and the publisher takes no responsibility for any of the statements.

ISBN : 978-81-8458-068-6

Laser typeset by **ISPCK,** Post Box 1585, 1654, Madarsa Road, Kashmere Gate, Delhi-110006.
Tel: 23866322/23
e-mail– ashish@ispck.org.in • ella@ispck.org.in
website-www.ispck.org.in

CONTENTS

FOREWORD ix
Introductory Note xi
Preface xiii
How do we use it? xix
Abbreviations xxv

PART ONE: CONFIRMATION

	I. *Christian Initiation*	**3-17**
Lesson 1:	Baptism	3
Lesson 2:	Confirmation: Laying-on-of-hands	8
Lesson 3:	Holy Communion	13
	II. *Christian Belief*	**19-30**
Lesson 4:	I believe in God the Father: The Creator	21
Lesson 5:	I believe in Jesus Christ: The Redeemer	25
Lesson 6:	I believe in the Holy Spirit: The Sanctifier	28
	III. *Christian Commitment*	**31-41**
Lesson 7:	Jesus Christ: Personal Lord and Saviour	33
Lesson 8:	Renouncing all that is Evil	36
Lesson 9:	Discipleship: Follower of Jesus Christ	39
	IV. *Christian 'Sadhna': Spiritual Discipline*	**43-60**
Lesson 10:	The Ten Commandments': Called to be Holy	45
Lesson 11:	The Holy Bible: The Word of God	49
Lesson 12:	The Lord's Prayer: Prayer and Worship	55

V. *Christian Fellowship*   61-71

Lesson 13:	The Church	63
Lesson 14:	Privileges and Duties	66
Lesson 15:	Vocation and Ministry	69

VI. *Christian Witness*   73-84

Lesson 16:	Go Forth into the World: Christian Home	75
Lesson 17:	Go Forth into the World: Christian Life and the Neighbour	79
Lesson 18:	Go Forth into the World: Christian Participation in Nation Building	82

PART TWO: BELIEVERS' BAPTISM   85-93

Lesson 1:	Baptism in the New Testament: Jewish Proselyte Baptism	87
Lesson 2:	Baptism in the New Testament: Baptism by John the Baptist	89
Lesson 3:	Baptism in the New Testament: As Received by our Lord Himself	90

> *Note:* Candidates for Believers' Baptism shall read **Part One**, beginning from Lesson 2 and **Part Two**, while Candidates for Confirmation shall read **Part One** Lessons 1 to 18. Part One covers (a) the main doctrines of the Christian Faith – explaining and expanding as necessary the Apostles' Creed; (b) the requirement of practical discipleship, including both the maintenance and growth of the devotional life and the application of faith to serve (*Ref.* A Pastor's Handbook for the Church of North India, pp. 30-31).

APPENDIX: 94-98

'The House of Worship of the Lord'   94

Dedicated

to

THE DIOCESE OF NORTH-EAST INDIA
(The Church of North India)

viii

Foreword

Our Christian life is a journey of Faith and Action. To enable us to walk this journey successfully for the glory of God, we need:-
   i.   the Grace of God;
   ii. instructions on our Faith and Beliefs;
   iii. the commitment to do or practice them.

It has been a long-felt need that the Church of North India provides a "tool" to its members to help and guide them in this endeavour of living, growing in and strengthening of our Christian life.

We praise God for all those whom He has chosen "from age to age", and for having "raised up prophets and wise men and women to point the way to him". The Church of North India would like to thank God, for Bishop Ernest W. Talibuddin who has received an urge from the LORD and also accepted the request of the CNI Synod to undertake this not-easy-task of preparing **A Handbook for Pastors' and Teachers', for Preparing Candidates for Confirmation and Believers' Baptism.**

Though, originally meant for the Diocese of North-East India, this handbook now comes as a blessing to the whole Church of North India. Our young people are our assets, who need to be nurtured, first "with milk" and then "with solid food" (Heb. 5:12-13). I am sure this handbook (translated later into other languages) will be used throughout our churches, as pastors' and teachers' "tend" and "feed" the flock of Christ. May this good work that Bishop Talibuddin has done bear fruit: 'Thirty, Sixty and a Hundred fold'.

– Rt. Rev. P. Lyngdoh,
Deputy Moderator, CNI

Bishop's Kuti,
Shillong - 1.

June, 2008

Introductory Note

It was a requirement of the Church of North India to have a guidebook for those preparing candidates for confirmation and believers' baptism with a proper theological base and with biblical teaching.

The Theological Commission thought about fulfilling this requirement and it had requested Bishop Ernest W. Talibuddin who has vast experience as a pastor, teacher and bishop to undertake the task of preparing this Handbook for Pastors' and Teachers'. He has gladly accepted this work and dedicated his time and energy to meet this urgent requirement of the CNI. We as the Church of North India are therefore very grateful to him for this labour of love.

The Theological Commission also felt that a section on the church building and the dress of the clergy should be included in the handbook, which is found here as well.

The Executive Committee of the CNI Synod in its 81st meeting appointed a committee consisting of the following members, Bishop V.M.Malaviya, Revd. Andrew Simick, Revd. Anita Templeton, Revd. P.S.Nag and Revd.Dr. Sunil M. Caleb, which has gone through the manuscript and approved it.

I am sure that this handbook will be of great help to those entrusted with preparing candidates for confirmation and for believers' baptism and I pray that the teaching of this book may be used for strengthening the unity, witness and service of the Church of North India.

We are most thankful for the encouragement and guidance provided by the Most Revd. Joel V. Mal, the Moderator of the CNI, Rt. Revd. P. Lyngdoh, Deputy Moderator, and the Revd. Dr. Enos Das Pradhan, General Secretary of the CNI Synod, and to ISPCK for the publication of this handbook.

Always be ready to make your defense to anyone who demands from you an accounting for the hope that is in you. (I Peter 3:15)

Ahmedabad, Gujarat **Bishop Vinod M. Malaviya**
September, 2008 *President,*
Theological Commission of the CNI

Preface

The Diocese of North-East India (CNI) is basically a rural diocese in a tribal context, although there are six congregations, which can be considered as urban or semi-urban. For practical and administrative reasons the diocese is divided into Deaneries, Pastorates and Congregations. A Pastorate is looked after by the Presbyter-in-Charge under whom there are several congregations scattered in an area of roughly one-hundred square kilometers or more. There are over three-hundred congregations. Most of them are scattered in the interior and remote areas. As far as I can recollect, the largest Pastorate has fifteen congregations and the smallest one has only five.

In most cases, the communication is very bad and almost throughout the year due to heavy rainfall the access to these congregations is not so easy.

Moreover, due to the shortage of ordained ministers, many of these congregations are looked after by the lay ministers – who are Lay-readers or Catechists – having neither any basic education, secular and religious, nor properly trained. But, they are sincere, dedicated and committed to the task they have been entrusted. The Presbyter-in-Charge in turn visits congregations in his Pastorate once in a month or once in two months for the celebration of the Lord's Supper, Solemnizing marriages, baptism, etc., and also to look into other pastoral and administrative matters. It is good and appreciable that a large number of lay-ministers are engaged in sharing the pastoral ministry of the church.

During my Episcopal ministry, I always made it a point to meet and examine the candidates a day before the **Confirmation**. Once, it was at All Saints' Church, Chabua, District Dibrugarh, Upper Assam, when I was examining the candidates, none of them came up to my expectation and satisfaction. The whole situation made me feel very unhappy. Next morning, I did not conduct the **Confirmation Service** for any of them. I am sure, not only the candidates, but their relatives and friends as well as the entire congregation must have been very upset and disappointed. However, I must also say that at least for the whole of next week, I too had an unpleasant state of mind and restless nights.

When I calmed down and reviewed the whole matter in its proper perspective, I realized that the **Confirmation** candidates were penalized for no fault of theirs, as they were not properly taught and prepared. So also, those who were responsible for preparing the candidates for **Confirmation** were helpless; as the required material was not available to them which they could use to execute their task.

The pertinent question that came to my mind was that at the local level who should provide the material? Obviously, it is the responsibility of the Presbyter-in-Charge and the Pastorate Committee. But, then, who should arrange such material for the Presbyters and the Pastorates in the diocese? Ultimately, it is the bishop, whose "office . . . is essentially a teaching office"[1] and of no one else. I asked God's pardon for the negligence on my part and took the whole responsibility upon myself as the bishop of the diocese.

I decided to prepare a *Handbook* for the pastors' and teachers' who prepare the candidates for **Confirmation**. Although, I had thought that I would be able to complete the

---

[1] *Part I, Chap. I, Sec. VIII, Sub-Section B, Clause 6* ©. **The Constitution of the Church of North India and Bye-Laws** as amended upto 9th October, 1986 (Green Book), Delhi: ISPCK, 1987, p. 25.

job before laying down my office as the Bishop of the Diocese of North-East India at the end of August, 1996 and making it a parting gift to the Diocese of North-East India; for various reasons, I could not even start the project immediately.

About seven or eight years ago, when I visited the Diocese of North-East India, Bishop Purely Lyngdoh, my worthy successor, shared his problem of lack of material for preparing candidates for **Confirmation**, and asked me to take up the project. Although, I began working on the project from then on, because of other priorities, I could not maintain the momentum.

It was the month of October, last year (2007), when I happened to be in the Office of the General Secretary, CNI Synod in New Delhi, he too encouraged me to take up the project and suggested that it should also cover the candidates for the **Believers' Baptism** (Adult Baptism). In fact, later on as per the decision of the CNI Synod Executive Committee (EC: 81:2008 – 147(a)), I have been officially requested to help "in preparing the lessons for **Confirmation** and **Adult Baptism** Classes." Although, I am privileged, I do feel too small to be asked to do this very important job for the whole of Church of North India.

Thus, what follows is due to the sense of responsibility that I still feel strongly as part of my *vocation* to help, particularly, the young people during the period of their spiritual nurture. It is also, due to the encouragement that I have received from two dear fellow servants in Christ, the Bishop of North-East India who is also the Deputy Moderator, CNI Synod and the General Secretary, CNI Synod. Because of the confidence that has been reposed in me by the CNI Synod Executive Committee, it encouraged me so much that I dared to take up the task of producing this *Handbook* as a humble contribution to the Church of North India in general, and the Christian youth in particular.

The *Handbook* is, primarily, aimed to help the pastors and the teachers to be equipped with material useful to them in their responsibility to prepare the candidates for **Confirmation** and **Believers' Baptism**. The *Lessons* are designed in such a way that they are flexible and adaptable, both, to the varied age groups as well as those who come from different academic and diverse social backgrounds. The main candidates are expected to come from rural or backward areas. If they are able to understand the fundamentals of their faith, then, no one else will have any problem. Thus, ultimately, it all depends upon the pastors and the teachers concerned as to how they would use these *Lessons* according to their need and context, helping the candidates to relate the teaching, which is basically biblical, to their everyday life. In other words, the intention is not to treat the candidates as theological students, but, to impart basic knowledge about Christian faith which everyone, who happens to be a *follower* of Jesus Christ, should reflect in his or her daily living. Jesus said, '*Let your light so shine before men, that they may see your good works and give glory to your Father who is in heaven*' (Mt. 5:16 RSV).

At the end of the *Lessons,* I have also, added as an *Appendix* on 'The House of Worship of the Lord', some information regarding church building and it has in it details of vestments, church's colours, etc.

In future, it is expected that the **Handbook** would be translated into Hindi, as well as other regional languages, which are commonly spoken among the people within the jurisdiction of the Church of North India, thus, making it available for use in the local congregations.

As mentioned earlier initially, the **Handbook** was aimed to meet the need of the Diocese of North-East India; it is now a humble gift from me as His servant to the Church of North India.

I would like to express my sincere thanks to Mrs. Neena Hemraj (my daughter) and Dipankar Soloman (my nephew) for reading the draft manuscript and making valuable comments; the Revd. (Dr.) R. George Michael, former Pro Vice-Chancellor, North-Eastern Hills University (NEHU), Shillong and Mrs. (Dr.) Prema Michael, former Professor of NEHU and Principal of Lady Doak College, Madurai for thoroughly reviewing and editing the final draft manuscript. A special word of gratitude to the Rt. Revd. Purely Lyngdoh, Bishop of North-East India & Deputy Moderator of the CNI Synod and the Rt. Revd. Vinod M. Malaviya, Bishop of Gujarat and President, CNI Synod Theological Commission for kindly having agreed to write a Foreword and an Introductory Note, respectively, for this *Handbook;* also, to Revd. Dr. Enos Das Pradhan, General Secretary, CNI Synod and Revd. Dr. Sunil M. Caleb, Principal, Bishop's College for kindly arranging a consultation in Kolkata (15-16th September, 2008) to give a final look at the manuscript and for extending all possible assistance enabling me to complete the task successfully. I also appreciate the valuable comments and suggestions made by the Revd. Andrew Simick, Presbyter-in-Charge, St. Paul's Cathedral, Kolkata. It was unfortunate that because of the bomb-blasts in New Delhi and attacks of Christians in Orissa, some other expected participants in the consultation could not come. We missed their wisdom and fellowship. My very special thanks to Mr. Himadri (Jim) S. De for kindly extending valuable help, unexpectedly, enabling me to complete the type-setting of the manuscript as per schedule.

I would fail in my responsibility if I do not express my thanks to Revd. Dr. Ashish Amos, Director & General Secretary, ISPCK, Delhi and his dedicated team for having readily agreed to publish the *Handbook* and that too before the 13th Ordinary Session of the CNI Synod so that it can be released during its meetings in October, this year.

Last but not least, Usha, my wife who always has been a great help, source of strength and encouragement all through my ministry – particularly, sharing and taking the responsibility of religious education.

Acharya +Ernest W. Talibuddin
September, 2008   INDORE – 452 010 (M.P.)

How Do We Use It?

It is one of the privileges for any pastor to prepare those already baptized for **Confirmation** or the adults for **Believers' Baptism**. It is also one of the most important tasks for the Presbyter-in-Charge of a given pastorate. The presbyter must take the maximum advantage of this opportunity. This is the occasion when a presbyter comes into the closest contact with the young members of the pastorate and, can exercise upon them his/her highest spiritual influence. This is the opportunity when a pastor can instruct them systematically about 'Christian belief, commitment, discipleship, fellowship and witness'. As a matter of fact, there cannot be any better opportunity for the pastor than this. It is one of the highest functions, the Presbyter-in-Charge has been called upon to, to get into a spiritual relationship with each of the candidates and lead them to experience the deeper things of religious life.

Preparing the candidates for **Confirmation** or **Believers' Baptism** serves one more purpose. It is an opportunity for the church to impart religious education to the young people after they have left Sunday School, usually, during the tender period of teen-age. A great deal depends on what the church attempts to do for its young people at that point. It is here that the preparatory classes should be conducted with much more care and devotion in a proper and systematic manner. There should not be any slackness on the part of the pastors' or teachers'. Each class should be regarded as a religious discipline.

Of course, there are practical difficulties as has been narrated earlier but, no Presbyter-in-Charge should pass on this most precious privilege as a shepherd of souls. In any case, the final responsibility lies with the Presbyter-in-Charge and therefore, he/she must direct the course of the preparation if some one is conducting the classes. Even then, he or she must arrange opportunities whereby a direct personal contact with the candidates is maintained.

I.

The classes must be conducted in a business like manner. Whether it is **Confirmation** or **Believers' Baptism**, it should not be done as a routine programme of the church. Instead, on one of the Sundays, in place of regular sermon, the Presbyter-in-Charge must give teaching on the subject of **Confirmation** or **Believers' Baptism** and thereby about the blessings of the rite. Thus, this will be for both the prospective candidates as well as their parents and elders in the families, so that they may question: 'Why should not I (or my son or daughter) be confirmed or baptized? It is only after this preliminary effort that their names should be enrolled for the classes. The attendance of the candidates must be marked regularly.

It is better to conduct classes separately for those who have been baptized as infants and have therefore grown up in the Christian tradition and, now wish to be confirmed. Likewise, another class, exclusively, for those who should be baptized as adults. Perhaps, it may be necessary to hold a few classes separately for boys and girls while giving teaching on matters related to gender issues. This will also offer an opportunity to discuss related personal matters freely. At this stage of their life, most of these young candidates pass through a period of biological change and physical growth. They also, begin to think and decide independently, which is the sign of gaining maturity. This is also the time when they become easily excited and passionate. It is therefore, essential that the pastors' and teachers' give a patient hearing. As a matter of fact, the young people should be encouraged to express themselves freely and particularly encouraged to ask their questions.

It must not be taken for granted that every young person born of Christian parents has been baptized. It is, therefore, the duty of the Presbyter-in-Charge to verify and check the Baptism Certificate whether the candidate has been baptized or not? A person can only be confirmed if he or she has already been baptized.

II.

'**Part One**' of the *Lessons* is primarily for **Confirmation** candidates. It has been structured on '**The Order of Confirmation**' of the Church of North India (*Ref.* The Book of Worship of the Church of North India, 1995, pp. 329-340).

'**Part Two**' of the *Lessons* is exclusively for candidates to be prepared for **Believers' Baptism** and are aimed at giving adequate instruction on the meaning of **baptism** (*Ref.* Pastor's Handbook for the Church of North India, 1983, pp. 30-31). **These candidates will read along with Part Two, Part One also, beginning from Lesson 2.**

III.

It is very important to understand that this is a *Handbook* for the pastors' and teachers' who prepare candidates for **Confirmation** and **Believers' Baptism** and **not** a '*text-book*' for the candidates. It is **not** a *Catechism* of olden days which the candidates were asked to learn by heart. The *Handbook* simply provides relevant material for pastors' and teachers' to base their teaching upon.

Thus, nothing should be read directly out of the *Handbook* during the class. Instead, the success of the teaching depends on the preparation of those who are responsible for preparing the candidates. Therefore, it is important that they must be clear about the biblical background of each *Lesson*. They must also adapt the *Lessons* according to the age, academic level and social background of the candidates.

It is also advisable that those who prepare the candidates use the Bible when conducting the classes. So also, every candidate – provided, *he* or *she* can read – should have a Bible of *his/her* own so that *he/she* may be taught how to refer to and encouraged to read the Bible everyday.

IV.

Adequate time should be given for preparing the candidates. In the olden days, the preparation for the **Confirmation** candidates used to take not less than six months. Even after such a long period of preparation, the candidates were not sure if they would be confirmed. In those days, the Bishop used to meet and examine each candidate normally a day before the **Confirmation.** If satisfied, only then, he would allow the candidate to be confirmed. Otherwise, he would simply say, 'My dear child, I will confirm you next time'. In one of the Anglican Parishes in Dublin, South Africa, the Parish Priest once told me, "preparation for the **Confirmation** candidates takes place for full three years: first year of systematic Bible study. Only those who pass the written examination on the Bible Study are allowed to go for **Confirmation** classes for the next two years." What a wonderful procedure!

The more important preparation above everything else is the spiritual preparation of the candidates themselves. Where the candidates are illiterate and naive, most of the time the preparation is often taken up for teaching verbally of the **Confirmation** or **Believers' Baptism** *Lessons*. In such cases, it is better to give spiritual instructions and leading the candidates out of a life of indifference and sin into a life of personal consecration and witness-bearing.

V.

Begin and conclude every session with prayer. Afterwards, since the expectant group of the candidates would be young and mostly in their teenage, it is better to create a warm atmosphere and start with some suitable jokes or stories. It helps a lot.

Each candidate, who is able to read and write should come to attend the classes with his or her own *Bible;* preferably, The Book of Worship (CNI) or a copy of the *CNI Order of Confirmation, A Form of Service for the Baptism of Children and Believers' Baptism, The Lord's Supper (CNI)* and *Morning and Evening Worship (CNI);* and a notebook and a pencil or ball pen.

> *The Pastors' and Teachers' responsible for preparing candidates for Confirmation or Believers' Baptism and wishing to use this Handbook must read this chapter on 'HOW DO WE USE IT?' carefully and follow as much as one can.*

Abbreviations

AD - anno Domino = In the year of our Lord
cf. - Confer (Latin) = compare
Chap. - Chapter
I Chron. - 1 Chronicles
Col. - Colossians
CNI - Church of North India
Cp. - Compare
I Cor. - 1 Corinthians
II Cor. - 2 Corinthians
Deut. - Deuteronomy
EC - Executive Committee
Eph. - Ephesians
Ex. - Exodus
Ezek. - Ezekiel
ff. - Following
Gal. - Galatians
Gen. - Genesis
Heb. - Hebrew
Hos. - Hosea
Ibid. - Ibidem = In the same book, chapter, passage
Is. - Isaiah
ISPCK - Indian Society for Promoting Christian Knowledge
Jas. - James
Jer. - Jeremiah
Jn. - John
I Jn. - 1 John
I Kgs. - 1 Kings
II Kgs. - 2 Kings
Lev. - Leviticus
Lk. - Luke
Mk. - Mark
Mt. - Matthew
Num. - Numbers
p. - page
I Pet. - 1 Peter
II Pet. - 2 Peter
Phil. - Philippians
pp. - pages
Prov. - Proverbs
Ps. - Psalm

Ref. – Reference
Rev. – Revelation
Rom. – Romans
RSV – Revised Standard Version
I Sam. – 1 Samuel
II Sam. – 2 Samuel
Sec. – Section
TV – Television
I Thess. – 1Thessalonians
I Tim. – 1Timothy
II Tim. – 2Timothy
Vs. – Verse
Vss. – Verses
Vv. – Verses
Zech. – Zechariah

PART ONE
Confirmation

I. *Christian Initiation*

2

Lesson 1

Baptism

Every organization or association has some system by which a person can become a member. However, because of their respective nature and function, the system often varies in every organization and association. Generally, such system requires payment of monthly or annual or life 'Membership Fee'; expects certain rules and regulations to be followed; and, in some cases, one has even to go through publicly some kind of act either by making a promise(s) or signing a declaration of intention or making some offering and so on.

According to several religious systems, to get *initiated* as their members, one has to go through such acts or rituals.

Question: What about Christianity?

Explanation: The Church too, has its own process to *initiate*[1] a person into its membership – such as a rite of the *Baptism*.

Question: What is Baptism?

Explanation: Ceremonial washing as a part of preparation to approach God in prayer and worship is a common feature of several religions – such as, Judaism (Lev. 8:6 & 14:9), Hinduism, Sikhism and Islam. Besides, thousands of Hindus, every year,

---

[1] *The Constitution of the Church of North India and Bye-Laws* (As amended up to 21st October,2005), Delhi: ISPCK, 2006, pp. 1-3.

make the journey to have a dip in River Ganges or Yamuna or any other river – 'which flow through our land bringing life, prosperity and cleansing to millions of people – stirring in their souls the longing for release from their sins and union with God'.[2]

As we go through the pages of the Old Testament, we find 'water appearing with great significance in many passages, which seem to pre-figure Christian *baptism* – such as, the Flood (Gen.7:17-8:5) brought death to wicked men and women but salvation to faithful Noah and his family. So also, the waters of the Red Sea were God's appointed means of deliverance and new life for the chosen people of God but destruction for their oppressors (Ex. 14:19-31). Naaman, suffering from leprosy found in the waters of the rather inferior River Jordan cleansing and new life (II Kgs. 5:1-15a)'[3].

The word *baptism* is derived from the Greek word *baptizein*, which simply means 'to dip into water to be cleansed from any kind of defilement'. In the time of our Lord, the custom was already in practice for those who wanted to adopt Jewish faith. They had to be not only circumcised but *baptized* to be 'born again' – the phrase that Saint Paul applied – a 'new creature' (II Cor. 5:17). The *baptism* of John was also according to this Jewish custom. It also differed from the ordinary ceremonial washing of the Jews, as it was not repeated. Instead, it was part of the preparation for the coming of the Kingdom of God (Mk. 1:2-4). In the New Testament, John is called *the Baptizer* (Mk. 1:4; 6:14 & 24) and *the Baptist* (Mk. 6:25, 8:28, Mt. 3:1, 11:1-12, 14:2 ,8, 16:14, 17:13, Lk. 7:20, 33 &9:19). Crowds 'were *baptized* by him in the river Jordan, confessing their sins' (Mk. 1:5). He preached 'the baptism of repentance' (Mk. 1:4).

---

[2] Bishop Christopher Robinson, *Christian Initiation: Thanksgiving of Parents after the Birth of a Child, Blessing of Children & Receiving a Catechumen*, (New Series No. 6), Delhi: ISPCK, May, 1987, p. 4.

[3] Bishop Christopher Robinson, *Believers' Baptism*, (New Series No. 7), Delhi: ISPCK, May, 1987, pp. 5-6.

Question: Since, Jesus was sinless, then, why did He receive the *baptism* of repentance from John?

Explanation: We read in all the four Gospels that Jesus received baptism from John (Mt. 3:13-17; Mk. 1:9-11; Lk. 3:21-22 & Jn. 1:31-34). At least four reasons seem evident: (1) to associate Himself with John the prophet who prepared the way for the Messiah; (2) to identify Himself with the sinful race He came to redeem; (3) to establish the course of His own ministry; and (4) to inaugurate His ministry officially.

Question: What is Christian Baptism?

Explanation: The 'Christian *baptism*, has always been associated with water' (Mk. 1:9-12; Jn. 3:1-8; Acts 8:26-40)[4]. It has been a natural symbol of purification. At Pentecost, Peter calls on all to 'repent and be baptized', in order to receive the promised gift of the Spirit (Acts 2:38). In a religious sense, therefore, it means:

a) 'a sign of cleansing from sins,
b) of engrafting into Christ,
c) of entrance into the covenant of grace, and
d) of fellowship with Christ in his death and resurrection and of rising to newness of life'.[5]

That is why for Paul it was *baptism* 'into Christ', i.e. into union with Him, into possession by him, into all benefits (Rom 6:4, I Cor. 1:13 & 12:13, Gal. 3:27). Although, the water in *baptism* certainly symbolizes the washing away of sin[6]; it almost means 'wash', in our sense of 'to wash oneself'. 'Moreover, it also links us first to the whole experience of the Exodus of the Israelites through the Red Sea (Ex. 13:17 – 14:31) – that is, from slavery in Egypt to freedom in the Promised Land'. In other

---

[4]*Ibid.*, p. 5.
[5]*CNI Constitution and Bye-Laws (As amended up to 21st October, 2005)*, Part I, Chapter I, Section V, Sub-Section A, Clause 2, p. 2.
[6]Bishop Christopher Robinson, *Op. cit.*, pp. 3-4.

words, it was an experience of 'from death to life'[7] (*Ref.* Ex. 14:13-14).

Paul reminds us, *"Do you not know that all of us who have been baptized into Christ Jesus were baptized into his death? We were buried therefore with him by baptism into death, so that as Christ was raised from the dead by the glory of the Father, we too might walk in newness of life. For if we have been united with him in a death like his, we shall certainly be united with him in a resurrection like his"* (Rom. 6:3-5 RSV).

This confirms that from the time of the apostles, *baptism* had become universal as the means of *entry* into the church and an *initiatory* rite and *sacrament* of the Christian Church.

Question: What is a sacrament?

Explanation: The word '*Sacrament*' in Latin means 'a sacred pledge'. However, the term '*sacrament*' came to be limited to those rites which were commanded in the New Testament. There 'are two *Sacraments* ordained by Christ our Lord in the Gospel, that is to say, *Baptism* and the *Supper of the Lord*. A *sacrament* is defined as 'an outward and visible sign ordained by Christ, of an inward and spiritual gift of God' – that is, 'grace' given to us. For example: In *baptism*, 'water' is an outward visible sign. The person is baptized '*In the name of the Father, and of the Son, and of the Holy Spirit'*, whereas, Saint Paul said, that baptism is a 'death unto sin, and a new birth unto righteousness; we are made the children of grace' (cf. Rom.6:4-6).

Question: What is required of a person to be *baptized*?

Explanation: Repentance! *John the baptizer appeared in the wilderness, preaching a baptism of repentance for the forgiveness of sins"* (Mk. 1:4 RSV).

---

[7]Bishop Christopher Robinson, *Ibid.*, pp. 3-4.

Question: At what age can a person be baptized?

Explanation: In the very early days of the church, the mission was mainly directed towards *adults*.[8] The process was as one single rite – that is: *the Baptism*, with the *gift of the Holy Spirit*, followed by the *first Communion*. This was because of practical contemporary needs; however, during the course of time it has changed.[9]

Although, in the very early days of the church, 'households were *baptized*, there is no indication whether these also included infants'. Nevertheless, 'on the strength of the idea in I Cor. 7:14, the infants probably were included'. The infants are *baptized* to be received into Christ's Church that they may grow up in grace and be trained in the household of faith. When they come of age, they are themselves bound to perform both, repentance and faith.

Question: What about *the baptism* in the Church of North India?

Explanation: 'The Church of North India believes that, while the operation of divine grace cannot be limited, the Sacraments of *Baptism* and *Holy Communion* were ordained by Christ Himself, as means of grace by which we are united to God and through which God works in us'.[10]

So also, 'In as much as the Church of North India will have within its membership both persons who practise *child's Baptism* in the sincere belief that this is in harmony with the mind of the Lord, and those whose conviction it is that the Sacrament can only properly be administered to a believer. Both, *Child Baptism* and *Believer's Baptism* shall be accepted as alternative practices in the Church of North India'.[11]

---

[8]*Op. cit.*, p. 2.
[9]*Op. cit.*, p. 2.
[10]*The Constitution of the Church of North India and Bye-Laws* (As amended up to 21st October, 2005), Part I, Chapter I, Section V, Delhi: ISPCK, 2006, p. 16.
[11]*Ibid.*, Clause 4, pp. 4-5.

Lesson 2

Confirmation
Laying-on-of-hands

We see that the *initiation* of a person into the life of the church is by means of *baptism* that has become universal, even from the time of the Apostles. We have also come to know that 'in the very early days of the church, *baptism* was being directly focused on the adults; initially, the process of *initiation* was one single rite: inclusive of *the Baptism*, *the Gift of the Holy Spirit*, and *the first Communion*.[12] But, later, during 'the course of time different practices grew up to meet practical contemporary needs which caused the one single act often to be divided into two or even three separate but connected acts': *The Baptism of Children* (Infant Baptism), followed later in life through *Confirmation* – by the Bishop – with the 'laying-on-of-hands', invoking *the Gift of the Holy Spirit*.[13]

Question: What is *Laying-on-of-hands*?

Explanation: Placing of one's hands – particularly, the hands of an elderly person- upon the head of another person is in many cultures – even, in Indian culture- considered a sign of blessing.

---

[12] Bishop Christopher Robinson, *Liturgical & Pastoral Notes: Christian Initiation* . . . (New Series No. 6), Delhi: ISPCK, May, 1987, p. 2
[13] *Ibid.*, pp. 2-3.

In the Old Testament, Jacob (Israel) blesses Joseph's sons (Gen.48:14ff) and Aaron blesses people (Lev. 9:22). In the New Testament, according to the custom, Jesus blesses the children (Mk. 10:13-16). Before His ascension into heaven, like Aaron, Jesus also *"lifting up His hands He blessed them (His disciples). While He blessed them, He parted from them"* (Lk. 24:50-51); but, there is no decisive evidence in the Scriptures that the '*Laying-on-of-Hands*' was commanded by Christ to be part of *baptism*.

However, 'there are few important passages bearing on the usage during the time of the Apostles: i) Acts 8:17 & 19: The Apostles *lay hands* on the newly-baptized Samaritan converts and the gift of the Holy Spirit is received. Here the '*Laying-on-of–hands*' follows *baptism*; ii) Acts 19:5-6: Paul baptizes and *lays hands* on the same people on the same occasion. The gift of the Spirit is given; iii) Hebrew 6:2: 'Teaching of *baptism* and *laying-on-of-hands*', most probably means the '*Laying-on-of-Hands*' which either accompanied or followed *baptism*; iv) Acts 13: 3; and v) (II Timothy 1:6; *cf*. I Timothy 5:14). In all these cases, the ceremony carries with it the receiving of the Holy Spirit and the appointment (or *ordination*) to some responsibility.

Question: What is *Confirmation*?

Explanation: We see that the '*Confirmation* is a rite that has come down to us from the time of the Apostles; whereby those who have been admitted to church membership by *baptism* are assured of, and through the rite of the *laying-on-of-hands,* are made partakers of the indwelling power of the Spirit of Pentecost who strengthens them (Acts 8:14-17 & 19:1-7, *cf*. Heb. 6:1-2; II Tim. 1:6; II Cor. 1:21 & I Jn. 2:20 & 27). These passages refer to a definite moment signifying some rite or ceremony at which the Holy Spirit was received by the believers.

Question: Then, what about the *Confirmation* in the church?

Explanation: In fact, 'all historic churches administer *Confirmation* and have administered it from the earliest times'.

The *Confirmation* is an important occasion in the life of a pastorate as the bishop of the diocese comes to confirm and preside over the Lord's Supper during which the newly confirmed make their *first communion*. But, for the *Confirmation* candidates it is a great and memorable day as it is once in a lifetime, a great milestone, which a baptized Christian passes on his or her pilgrimage for the rest of life in this world to heaven.

As a matter of fact, the *'Confirmation* is one of the three services we go through once in a lifetime. The other two are: *Baptism* and the *Burial of the Dead'*.

Question: What is required of those who are to be *confirmed*?

Explanation: At the very beginning of the Confirmation service (CNI Sect. 4) the Bishop invites all, 'Let us first confess our sins in penitence and faith . . . '. Thus, the first and foremost requirement of those to be confirmed is that they should have the experience of repentance and faith, by which they are ready to receive the Holy Spirit.

In the simplest possible way, it can be described as an occasion for those baptized to *Publicly Profess their Faith* and declare their desire to be confirmed (*see CNI Order of Confirmation, General Rubrics 2-4, pp. 4 & 5*) In doing so, they are also *confirming* by giving their own assent to the pledge, which was made at their *baptism* by those who had brought them for *baptism* to be nurtured in the Christian faith in God, the Father, the Son and the Holy Spirit (*see CNI Order of Confirmation Section 7*). Thus, the candidate does three things: 'Professes Personal Discipleship', 'Declares his/her Faith in the Lord Jesus Christ, and 'Makes the Promises'.

The bishop, then, *lays his hand* upon the candidate in accordance with the practice of the Apostles (Acts 8:14-17 & 19:1-7) and prays that the Holy Spirit may strengthen him/her to *follow* Christ and to be His faithful *witness* (*see CNI Order of Confirmation, Sec. 7*). Also, in his prayer, bishop prays:

"Strengthen, O Lord, your child/servant that... (he/she) may continue to be yours forever, and daily grow in your Holy Spirit more and more until (he/she) comes to your everlasting kingdom" (*See CNI Order of Confirmation, Sec. 24*). However, we must remember that the bishop's hand is but an earthly symbol of the fatherly hand of God which always guides and holds His children. Thus in a way, the '*Confirmation*' is both an opportunity to confirm as well as to be confirmed.

Question: What about *Confirmation* in the Church of North India?

Explanation: Let us take note of the full title as has been written in the Book of Worship of the Church of North India (*p.325*): '*The Order of Confirmation with the Public Profession of Faith of those Baptized as children and Reception into Communicant Membership of the Church*'. Thus, "this means that the form of admission into communicant membership of the CNI is either through *Confirmation* by a Bishop or through "some such service" conducted either by a Bishop or Presbyter.

The candidates give their own assent to the pledge, as they do not '*confirm*', but the Bishop does. The candidates *are confirmed*. This distinction is very important as the purpose of *Confirmation* is not the renewal of the baptismal vows. Although, the title of the Book of Worship of the Church of North India reads (p.325): '*The Order of Confirmation with the Public Profession of Faith . . . and Reception into Communicant Membership of the Church*'; we must 'not make the mistake of identifying *Confirmation* with a ceremony of admission to Holy Communion. But, *Confirmation* has an important function in itself – that is, to make the individual Christian a partaker of the gift of Pentecost. Of course, a person who has sought the strengthening by the Holy Spirit needs to be constant in that strength through fellowship with Christ and a solemn participation in that sacrament. For many of us the Holy Communion is one of the most helpful means of renewing that fellowship'.

Question: What is the relation of Baptism to Confirmation?

Explanation: Although, 'in Apostolic times *Baptism* also included a *Laying-on-of-Hands* (Acts 19:6, cf. Heb. 6:2) and possibly an anointing with oil (II Cor.1:21-22; I Jn. 2:20 & 27); as far as the relation of *Baptism* to *Confirmation* is concerned, as already has been pointed out earlier, there is 'no decisive evidence in Scripture that the *laying-on-of-hands* was commanded by Christ'. In the Book of Acts of the Apostles, we read *"Now when the apostles at Jerusalem heard that Samaria had received the word of God, they sent to them Peter and John, who came down and prayed for them that they might receive the Holy Spirit; for it had not yet fallen on any of them, but they had only been baptized in the name of the Lord Jesus. Then they laid their hands on them and they received the Holy Spirit"* (Acts 8:14-17 cf. 19:1-7).

Thus, '*Baptism* is the first and *Confirmation* is the second step in *initiation* into the church'. Since, 'the *Confirmation* is the second step in initiation into the church, it is important to be certain beyond all doubt that *Confirmation* candidates have been baptized. *Baptism* places a person within the church, and it is absolutely necessary before a person can receive any other sacrament of the church, either, *Confirmation* or *Holy Communion*'.[14] 'It is in *Baptism* either in infancy or as adult that a person is incorporated into the body of Christ'[15] (Gal. 3:27) and it places a person within the church. *Baptism* is a sign of cleansing from sin, whereas, *Confirmation* is the public profession of those baptized. That is why the precondition for those who desire to be confirmed is that they first have to be baptized. Moreover, 'the grace of *Confirmation* is in some sense the gift of the Holy Spirit to be strengthened'.

---

[14] *A Pastors Handbook for the Church of North India*, Delhi: ISPCK, 1983, p. 45 – (*See* CNI Constitution, Part I, Chapter I, Section II, Sub-Section A, Clause 1 and Sub-Section B, Clause 5).

[15] Cf. *The Book of Worship of the Church of North India*, Delhi: ISPCK, 1995, pp. 303-304.

Lesson 3
Holy Communion

All over the world, it is something common to express fellowship with one another by sharing a common meal. Often, these common meals have religious significance. As far as the fellowship between Christians is concerned its chief expression is in the *Holy Communion* service.

In an earlier *Lesson*, we saw that during the course of time different practices grew up to meet practical contemporary needs which caused the *Baptism* – as a single rite for *initiation* – divided into the *Baptism of Children* (Infant Baptism), followed by later in life by *Confirmation* – generally administered by the Bishop – with *'Laying-on-of-Hands'*, invoking the gift of the Holy Spirit. Then, this was followed – either immediately or shortly afterwards – by the *first reception of Holy Communion*.

Question: What is *Holy Communion*?

Explanation: *Holy Communion* is one of the two sacraments that Christ Himself ordained (Mt. 26:26-28; Mk. 14:22-24; Lk. 22:17-19; I Cor. 11:23-25 & 10:16). The other one is *Baptism*. If, in *Baptism* the outward and visible sign is 'water', which stands for 'heavenly washing' and cleansing through the blood of Christ; in *Holy Communion* the outward and visible sign is 'bread' and 'wine' exhibiting the giving of His body and blood in death on the cross and our personal share in what He has done for us. Hence, it is the central service of the church. In the Book of Acts of the Apostles we read that "*all who believed were together . . . breaking the bread in their homes . . .*" (Acts 2:44-46 RSV).

It is here – in the *Holy Communion* – first we hear His living voice when His written *word* is read and expounded; and, then we have *His Presence* in our midst to make Himself known to us through the *'breaking of the bread'* as He did to those on the road to Emmaus (Lk. 24:13-35, *Ref.* vss. 30 & 31 RSV).

Question: What is the place of *Holy Communion* in *Christian Initiation*?

Explanation: Let us not forget that in the early church, *Holy Communion* used to be the last of the three acts of one single rite of *Believer's Baptism*. It used to follow after *Confirmation*. The Orthodox Church still preserves it as one single unbroken rite. In some other church traditions, the sequence of the original single service has been retained unbroken, even if the three parts have been separated by a period of time.[16]

It has already been noted earlier that, 'The form of admission into communicant membership shall be through *Confirmation* by a bishop or through some such service conducted by a bishop or presbyter.'[17] The admission of the newly confirmed is sealed by the reception of the *Holy Communion*.[18]

Question: As *Lord's Supper*, what are other significances of this sacrament?

Explanation: Saint Paul, who is the writer of the two letters to the church of God at Corinth (I Cor. 1:2), calls it the *Lord's Supper*

---

[16] Bishop Christopher Robinson, Ed., *Christian Initiation* (New Series No. 6), May 1987, pp. 2-3.
[17] *A Pastor's Handbook for the Church of North India*, Delhi: ISPCK, 1983, p.54.
[18] *Ibid.*, p. 54.

(I Cor. 11:20) as it is the *fellowship* meal of Christians. *"Because there is one loaf, we who are many are one body, for we all partake of the same loaf"* (I Cor. 10:17). It is the sign of the bond among believers.

According to Saint Paul, *'the Lord Jesus on the night when he was betrayed took bread, and when he had given thanks, he broke it, and said, "This is my body which is for you. Do this in remembrance of me." In the same way also the cup, after supper, saying, "This cup is the new covenant in my blood. Do this, as often as you drink it in remembrance of me"'* (I Cor. 11: 23b-25 RSV). Thus, the sacrament of the *Lord's Supper* is a 'continual *remembrance* of the sacrifice of the death of Christ, and of the benefits which we receive thereby'. When Paul said, *"For as often as you eat this bread and drink the cup, you proclaim the Lord's death until he comes"* (I Cor. 11:26 RSV); He meant it also to be a commemoration. Thus, the service is *communion* as well as *commemoration*.

The *Lord's Supper* is also called *'the Eucharist"* (in Greek) which means *"thanksgiving"*. It is we who give our thanks to God for Christ's wonderful love and death for us, for the benefit of our share in His death and for our fellowship together which is based upon it.

Question: What about *Holy Communion* in the Church of North India?

Explanation: First, 'The Church of North India believes that, while the operations of divine grace cannot be limited, the Sacraments of *Baptism* and the *Holy Communion* were ordained by Christ Himself, as means of grace by which we are united to God and through which God works in us'.[19]

---

[19] *The Constitution of the Church of North India and Bye-Laws* (as amended up to 21st October, 2005), Part I, Chap. I., Sec. V, Clause 1, Delhi: ISPCK, 2006, p. 16.

'The Church of North India recommends that every service of *Holy Communion* include the following elements:

a) Thanksgiving for God's glory and goodness with the expression of penitence and prayer that all may communicate worthily;

b) Communication of Christ's life and work through the ministry of the Word and through the recitation of the Creed;

c) Intercession for the church and the world;

d) Showing forth and pleading before the Father, Christ's sacrifice once for all offered, invoking Christ's merits for the whole church, remembering His resurrection and ascension and the outpouring of the Holy Spirit, who continuously indwells and inspires the church and looking forward to Christ's coming again in glory;

e) Presenting ourselves, our souls and bodies, as a living sacrifice to God;

f) Communion and fellowship with God, with one another and with the people of God on earth and with all the company of heaven; and,

g) Offering to God our sacrifice of praise and thanksgiving for the grace received in *Holy Communion*'.[20]

Question: What is required of those who come to the *Lord's Supper*?

Explanation: When we are invited for a dinner by some friend, how much preparations do we make? The first and the foremost is as to how best we can present ourselves – in our outlook, behaviour, manners, etc., – Secondly, how best to enjoy the feast and the fellowship? Since, the *Lord's Supper* is the 'Supper of the Lord', then, how much preparation for our participation is needed so that we can fully enjoy the benefit of both the feast and the fellowship and get spiritually nourished.

---

[20]*Ibid.*, Sub-Sec. B, Clause 16, pp.19-20.

Thus, the first requirement is to examine ourselves. It is easy to remember all the bad things we did during the previous week and we ask God to forgive. But equally, there are also good things we have failed to do. We must also ask God for His forgiveness. We should be thankful to Jesus for His death for us.

But, there is always a condition attached to God's forgiveness: In absolution, the Presbyter pronounces, 'Almighty God, who forgives all who forgive one another and truly repent of their sins . . . '[21] Jesus said, *'if you are offering your gift at the altar, and there remember that your brother has something against you, leave your gift there before the altar and go; first be reconciled to your brother (or sister), and then come and offer your gift'* (Mt. 5:23-24 RSV)

We, therefore, place our intention in humility, before God to be in charity with all henceforth.

---

[21]*The Book of Worship of the Church of North India: An Order for the Lord's Supper or The Holy Eucharist,* Delhi: ISPCK, 1995, p. 115.

II. *Christian Belief*

Lesson 4

I Believe in God, the Father
The Creator

It has already been said in the introduction, that the purpose of these *Lessons* is not to make all of you (candidates) theologians but to help you to understand in the simplest possible way what you *believe* as a *follower* of Jesus Christ. As a matter of fact, it is important for every Christian to understand what he or she *believes* in and why he or she *believes* it? Merely reciting the *Creed* means nothing.

There are many who live a good life but they do not *believe* in Jesus Christ. Even Saint Paul himself said that, he was '*a persecutor of the church, as to righteousness under the law, blameless*' (Phil. 3:6). Thus, as someone has said, 'It is not behaviour that makes a Christian but *belief*. Behaviour follows'. Saint John tells us, "*For God so loved the world that he gave his only begotten Son, so that everyone who believes in him may not perish but may have eternal life.*" (Jn. 3:16 RSV).

Question: What is Christian Belief?

Explanation: The word "creed" is derived from the Latin verb *credo,* which means '*I believe*'. That is why the "creed" begins with these words. There are two main versions of Christian creed: The *Apostles' Creed* and the *Nicene Creed*. They are summaries of *Christian Belief*.[22] Both 'the *Creeds* consist of simple statements without explanation or argument. They assert simple facts of history and theology'. In other words, they are the public profession of faith in Christ. In the western church, it was the custom to begin the *Creed* with "*I believe*"; whereas, in the eastern churches it begins, "*We believe*". The West emphasizes the personal element in faith; the East emphasizes the corporate aspect as for them, faith is a common faith.

Question: Why is one of the *Creeds* called the *Apostles' Creed*?

Explanation: The *Apostles' Creed* was not composed by the twelve apostles. It is called the *Apostles' Creed* because it states concisely the teaching which the apostles gave us in the New Testament about God. In fact, it took its present form by the middle of the eighth century A.D. In the early days, each church had a short summary of the main points of *belief* which served as a syllabus for those who were preparing the catechumens (convert under instruction before *baptism*), for *Baptism* was to be used by them as a form in which they professed their faith. Originally, this was the *baptismal creed* of the Church of Rome.

Question: What about the *Nicene Creed*?

Explanation: The *Nicene Creed* is also one of those *baptismal creeds* and most probably of the church at Jerusalem. This expanded version, on one hand, aimed to make the *Christian belief* more understandable to ordinary people and on the other, it became a witness to the faith of the church against false teaching. Consequently, this became the statement of faith of the whole Catholic (This does not mean Roman Catholic) Church which has been handed down to us. This expanded *Creed* was accepted by the First General Council of the Church held at Nicea in AD 325. Therefore, it is called *Nicene Creed*.

---

[22] Part I, Chap. I, Sec. III, Clause 3 & 4, *The Constitution of the Church of North India and Bye- Laws (as amended up to 21st October, 2005)*,Delhi: ISPCK, 2006, pp. 4-5.

Question: What does it mean, '*I believe in God, the Father*'?

Explanation: If we just say, "*I believe*", then, it would simply mean that 'I am of an opinion of . . .' But, then, what opinion? If we say, '*I believe in God, the Father*'; it does make sense. Although, all – adherents of other religious faiths – use the word 'God' in its different forms and meaning; it is only the Christian who can say with confidence that, '*I believe in God, the Father . . . Creator of . . .*'. Jesus said, '*When you pray, go into your room and shut the door and pray to your Father who is in secret; and your Father who sees in secret will reward you . . . your Father knows what you need before you ask him. Pray then like this: "Our Father who art in heaven . . ."* (Mt.6:6-9 RSV) – A very personal relation with God is implied.

The *Christian belief* is a complete trust in God as a real Person. All through the Scripture, God is represented as a 'Personal' God. Thus, it is committing oneself to Him as well as establishing personal relationship with Him, who is *One*. 'There are two kinds of unity: "mathematical" and "organic". A "mathematical" unity is one and indivisible; whereas, an "organic" unity may contain many component parts. God's unity is "organic". Although, He is *One,* His unity comprises the *Father,* the *Son* and the *Holy Spirit.*

This is also what we mean by *Trinity:* Three Persons – "tri" and "unity" – that is, God is both, three and one. Each of these Persons has a distinct character. Though it may not be very appropriate, let me give an example to explain. Water is liquid. It has its own properties, but when it is frozen it becomes solid and properties change. It can be used differently. Likewise, when water is boiled, it takes the form of steam and its properties change.

God is the Father – this asserts that He is personal and thus primarily 'loves' – He is the *Creator* of the world. The Holy Bible begins with this statement, "*In the beginning God created the heavens and the earth . . .* " (Gen.1:1 RSV). The psalmist says, "*The heavens are telling the glory of God; and the firmament proclaims his handiwork"* (Ps. 19:1); Saint Paul also says, *"Ever since the creation of the world his invisible nature, namely, his eternal power and deity, has been clearly perceived in the things that have been made . . . "* (Rom. 1:20). Again, while addressing the people in Athens, Saint Paul proclaims, " . . . *he himself gives to all men life and breath and everything"* (Acts 17:25).

Often, there is an argument that 'if God is *Almighty*, why does He allow evil?' The answer is that He is first of all a *Father*. Therefore, He does not impose His power rather He wants us to *choose* to be good. Because *'God is love'* (I Jn. 4:8 & 16) and *'love'* is not love unless it is free (Hos.14:4).

Lesson 5

I Believe in Jesus Christ
The Redeemer

In the previous *Lesson*, we focused on the first paragraph of the Creed which simply deals with *'God the Father'*. Now, we come to the second paragraph, which also begins, 'I believe *in Jesus Christ'*[23]. It concerns *Christian belief* in *Jesus Christ*, which on the one hand binds His *followers* together all over the world, and on the other hand, separates them from the rest of the world.

Question: Who is Jesus Christ?

Explanation: Jesus wrote no autobiography nor did He leave anything in writing. Strictly speaking, even the Gospels are not biographies at all. They are 'memoirs', selected historical reminiscences; of course, with a purpose: "*These are written that you may believe that Jesus is the Christ, the Son of God, and that believing you may have life in his name*" (Jn. 20:31 RSV). He simply committed Himself and His teaching to the hearts and memories of the people who knew and loved Him.

According to the second paragraph of the Apostles' Creed, which reads, '*And in Jesus Christ, his only Son, our Lord . . .*'[24] Saint Luke tells us that, '*At the end of the eight days, when he was*

---

[23] *The Book of Worship of the Church of North India*, Delhi: ISPCK, 1995, pp. 7-8.
[24] *Ibid.*, p. 7.

circumcised, he was called Jesus, the name given by the angel before he was conceived in the womb' (Lk. 2:21 RSV). The Hebrew word for it is Jehoshua (=Joshua), which means 'Jehovah is salvation' (Num. 13:16). Since, he was named *Jesus* when eight days were fulfilled for circumcising Him, the name therefore, reminds us that He was one of the seeds of Abraham and thus, belonged to the race that God had chosen to be the agent of His mission.

Christ is a Greek word which means the 'Anointed' or the 'Messiah' in Hebrew. It is a title and not a proper name. In Israel, in early times, high priests (Ex.29:7) and kings were anointed with oil as a sign that God had chosen them for their offices. Anointing had to do with being set apart and being given power. Jesus never openly claimed to be the Messiah. In fact, when Peter declared him to be the *Christ*, Jesus' response was to charge his disciples to tell no one about Him (Mk. 8:29f. *cf.* Lk. 9:20f.).

In the Old Testament we find God's relation to His Chosen People, Israel, as His Son (Ex. 4:22-23 *cf.* Hos. 11:1). Thus, the fatherhood of God and sonship of *Jesus Christ* is not based on physical relationship, but on the love of God for His people. It is entirely a moral and spiritual relationship. As regard to 'father-son relationship' see the Second Book of Samuel (II Sam. 7, 13 & 14 *cf.* Ps. 89:26 & 27). In Psalm 2, for the first time the term 'begotten' was used in this connection. In the New Testament, Saint Mark begins, 'The Gospel according to Mark': *"The beginning of the gospel of Jesus Christ, the Son of God'* (Mk. 1:1 RSV).

At His Baptism and Transfiguration, the voice said, *"Thou art my beloved Son; with thee I am well pleased"* (Mk. 1:11 RSV) and *"This is my beloved Son; listen to Him"* (Mk. 9:7 RSV). Here, *'beloved Son'* meant an *'only son'*. The beloved Son is also the *only begotten Son*. Nevertheless, we too are sons and daughters of God, for we are taught by Jesus to pray, *'Our Father'* (Lk. 11:2-4). Saint Paul makes it clearer, *'for in Jesus Christ you all are sons (and daughters) of God, through faith . . . '* (Gal. 3:26-28 & 4:4 RSV).

The Nicene Creed makes it clear that 'Jesus was eternally begotten of the Father. Thus, deriving His being from God, He is "of one substance with the Father" (Jn. 1:18), begotten before the worlds. Although He was born into this world as other babies are born, He was a perfect Man, of the substance of His mother. Yet, He was 'conceived by the Holy Spirit' (*Ref.* Lk. 1:35), simply "clothed with flesh".

Question: 'The Redeemer'. What does it mean?

Explanation: Redemption is the deliverance from some evil or bondage by payment of a price or ransom. According to the Old Testament law, the owner of a dangerous animal could be executed if the animal gored someone to death, but he could redeem his life by paying a ransom. This concept was taken up by the early Christians to describe the work of Christ, who gave his life 'as a ransom for many' (Mk. 10:45; Mt. 20:28). Sinful people are in bondage to sin (Jn.8:34) for which death is the only possible consequence (Rom. 6:23). The cross of Christ is the price paid to release the slaves and to let the condemned prisoners go free. The price is Christ's shed blood (Eph. 1:7; *cf.* I Cor. 6:19ff.). Thus, it is Christ who is the *Redeemer*. It also indicates that the reality of sufferings is an essential part of Christian faith. If we have never faced the implication of the words, "*He suffered*", then, there is no cross in our lives.

Question: What is the position of the Church of North India as regard to Jesus Christ as *Redeemer*?

Explanation: 'The Church of North India holds the faith which the church has ever held in Jesus Christ the Redeemer of the world, in whom alone persons are saved by grace through faith. In accordance with the revelation of God, He made Himself God incarnate. It worships one God – the Father, Son and the Holy Spirit'.[25]

---

[25] Part I, Chap. I, Sec. III, Clause 1, *The Constitution of the Church of North India and Bye-Laws as amended up to 21st October, 2005),* Delhi: ISPCK, 2006, p. 4.

Lesson 6

I Believe in the Holy Spirit
The Sanctifier

We have now come to the third paragraph of the *Creed* which concerns the *Holy Spirit*. Although, sometimes described as the neglected Person of the *Trinity*; still by its threefold division, the *Creed* places the *Holy Spirit* on exactly the same level as *the Father* and *the Son*. This asserts by implication the truth of His divinity also. He is called *the Spirit* because He is (like God the Father) a spiritual Being, who (unlike the Lord Jesus) never had a body.

The *Apostles' Creed* introduces simply by saying '*I believe in the Holy Spirit*'; but, the Nicene Creed describes Him as, '*We believe in the Holy Spirit, the Lord, the giver of life . . . '*.

Question: Who is the *Holy Spirit*?

Explanation: As we read the Old Testament, we find God the Father revealing Himself. So also, when we read the New Testament, in the Gospels we see Jesus Christ being portrayed.

In Nazareth, when in a synagogue, Jesus read from the book of the Prophet Isaiah, "*The Spirit of the Lord is upon me, because he has anointed me . . .* "(Is. 60:1a RSV); He was saying that His power was the power of God the *Holy Spirit* resting upon Him (*cf.* Lk. 4:18a RSV). And He also told His disciples that when He left them, the same *Holy Spirit* would come upon them to be their power (*cf.* Acts 1:8). Consequently, this is exactly what happened on the day of Pentecost. The God who had been *alongside* the disciples in the Person of God the Son, entered them in the Person of God the *Holy Spirit*.

When we go through the pages of the Acts of the Apostles, the Acts were of the *Holy Spirit* through the apostles. The epistles also disclose more of *His* work. In fact, the life of every Christian and the life of the church as a whole depend on the gracious presence and activity of the *Holy Spirit*. Thus, the truth is that at every point, we are dependent upon the *Holy Spirit*.

The Name which Jesus gave to the *Holy Spirit* is "Paraclete", which means one called alongside to help, advocate, helper, strengthener, fortifier and comforter (Jn.14:16). A Church without the *Holy Spirit* is not a Christian Church at all (Rom. 8:9). So also every true Christian Church is a Trinitarian Church, God the Father, God the Son and God the Holy Spirit.

Question: What does it mean by *God the Holy Spirit* as 'Sanctifier'?

Explanation: In the Old Testament, the Hebrew root word has two basic meanings: 'set apart for exclusive use', 'separated', 'regarded as sacred'; or it can mean 'brightness', an idea related to *purification*. But, '*sanctification*' could be simply external with a deeper inner reality, whereas God requires a moral response from His people reflecting His righteousness (Dt. 4:6 *ff.*).

In the New Testament, the emphasis is on inward transformation leading to *purity* of thought and deed expressed in lives of goodness and godliness (*cf.* Mt. 23:17*ff* & Jn. 17:17*ff.*). The *Holy Spirit* works through the believer's faithful dependence upon Him to produce increasing spiritual maturity.

As a matter of fact, 'God's ideal for us is absolute holiness'. Jesus said, "*You . . . must be perfect, as your heavenly Father is perfect*" (Mt. 5:48 RSV). Although we are judged at the end by our works (II Cor. 5:10, etc), good works are the necessary fruit of that life lived in union with God of which justification is the initial act (*cf.* Mt. 7:16-30). Because Christ died not only to save us from the punishment of sin, but from sin itself. 'He died to make us good'. Through the *Holy Spirit* He imparts to us His own perfect human nature. The will of God is our *sanctification* (I Thess. 4:1-8), the complete subjection of all our powers of will and heart and mind to God's *Holy Spirit* (*cf.* Mt. 22:37).

'Our growth in holiness may be called either as the work of Christ or of the *Holy Spirit*. That is why at the *Confirmation*, the Bishop lays his hand on the head of each candidate and prays, '*Strengthen, O Lord, your child/servant . . . with your Holy Spirit*'[26]

Jesus said, "*I will pray the Father, and he will give you another Counsellor, to be with you forever, even the Spirit of truth, whom the world cannot receive, because it neither sees him nor knows him; you know him, for he dwells with you, and will be in you . . . I will not leave you desolate: I will come to you*" (Jn14:16-18 RSV)'. Thus, it is through the Spirit that the Ascended Lord dwells in the church and operates in believers (Rom. 8:1-17 *cf.* Acts 1:1-8; 2:1-47; 4:1-35; 8:4-17; 9:1-20;10:1-48; 19:1-7; Lk. 11:9-13; Gal. 5:18-15 & Is. 11: 1-2).

Question: What is the position of the Church of North India regarding *God the Holy Spirit* as '*Sanctifier*'?

Explanation: 'The Church of North India holds the faith which the church has always held in Jesus Christ the redeemer of the world, in whom alone persons are saved by grace through faith, and in accordance with the revelation of God, Himself being God Incarnate. It worships one God – the Father, the Son and the Holy Spirit'.[27]

---

[26] The Order of Confirmation . . . Sect. 23, *The Book of Worship of the Church of North India*, Delhi: ISPCK, 1995, p.337.

[27] Part I, Chap. I, Sec. III, Clause 1, *The Constitution of the Church of North India and Bye-Laws* (as amended up to 21st October, 2005), Delhi: ISPCK, 2005, p. 4.

III. *Christian Commitment*

Lesson 7

Jesus Christ
Personal Lord and Saviour

In the Indian context, which is religiously pluralistic – where Christianity is one among several other religious faiths, such as: Hinduism, Buddhism, Jainism, Judaism, Islam, Zoroastrianism and Tribal religions – it is very important to understand as to what it is that is unique in Christianity and that why we are Christians? Different people think differently. Some think of it in terms of *believing its creed* or *adopting and adhering to the Christian code* strictly. For some, however, it is merely to *observe Christian Feasts and Festivals and ceremonies* – particularly participating in Worship on Sundays regularly and on other important days – For others, it is active participation in its programmes and extending financial help and support. Of course, while these things are important, they are not enough to make someone a genuine and *committed* Christian.

Christianity is neither a creed nor a code nor ceremonies. It is not even a religion of a book. Instead, it is a *Person*. In other words, 'Christianity is Christ'. As Saint Paul says, *"For no other foundation can any one lay than that which is laid, which is Jesus Christ"* (I Cor. 3:11 RSV). Therefore, Christ has to be the centre of our life, both in terms of what we believe and how we behave.

Question: What does it mean by *Christian Commitment*?

Explanation: The English word *commitment* simply means 'engagement that restricts freedom of action'. In other words, it means to be a *'slave'* or *'bondservant'*. *'Slavery'* was a familiar feature of life even in the ancient world.

It is interesting to note that in the New Testament, Paul, Peter, James and Jude begin their letters by describing themselves as "a slave or bondservant of Jesus Christ" (Rom. 1:1, Phil. 1:1; II Pet. 1:1; Jas. 1:1 & Jude 1:1). They knew that Jesus Christ had bought them at the cost of His life blood and that as a consequence they belonged to Him and were entirely at His service. This explains the paradox of *Christian Commitment* as Paul describes himself a slave of Jesus Christ which demands *unflinching* loyalty.

That is why one of the first things that the Bishop asks the candidates is to declare their acceptance of Jesus Christ as their *Lord* and *Saviour*, and their *commitment* to Him forever.

Saint Peter concludes his second letter with the following words of affirmation; *'But grow in the grace and knowledge of **our** (Personal)* **Lord** *and* **Saviour** *Jesus Christ* (II Pet. 3:18a RSV).

Question: *'Jesus* Christ as *Personal Lord* and *Saviour':* What does it mean?

Explanation: The primary meaning of *Lord* is 'ruler' or 'commander' and often means the 'master' of a slave. The same word is also used in speaking of, or to God in the Old Testament.

The earliest, shortest and simplest of all Christian *creeds* was the affirmation *'Jesus is Lord'* (Acts 10:36; Rom. 10:9 & I Cor. 12:5) Those who acknowledged His *lordship* were baptized and received into the Christian community. Paul wrote, *'if you confess with your mouth, "Jesus is Lord," and believe in your heart that God raised Him from the dead, you will be saved'* (Rom.10:9). He also wrote, *'no one can say "Jesus is Lord" except by the Holy Spirit'* (I Cor. 12:3). He is the sovereign ruler of the universe and of the church (Col. 2:9). Thus, Jesus Christ's title *'Lord'* is the recognition of His victory over all the forces of evil that have been put under His feet (I Cor. 15:27a & Eph. 1:22).

The earliest Christian *creed*, '*Jesus is Lord*' takes us to the second affirmation that He is '*Saviour*'. Saint Paul says, '*every one who calls upon the name of the Lord will be saved*' (Rom. 10:13 RSV).

In the Old Testament the word '*saviour*', is used as a title applied to successful captains (Judges 3:9), kings (II Kings 13:5), etc. But, ultimately, it was God who raised up the *saviours* for the nation in time of need and was thought of as *the Saviour* (Ps. 106:21; Is. 43:3 &11).

In the New Testament there are 24 instances of the use of the word, '*saviour*'. About one-third of these references to the title speak of Christ as a *saviour* from human's worst enemy – that is 'sin' (Jn. 4:42; I Tim. 1:10; I Jn. 4:14). In the Gospel according to St. Matthew, we read, '*an angel of the Lord appeared to Joseph in a dream, saying, "Joseph, son of David, do not fear to take Mary your wife, for that which is conceived in her is of the Holy Spirit; she will bear a son, and you shall call his name Jesus, for he will save his people from their sins"*' (Mt. 1:20-21 RSV).Thus, it is an affirmation that contains within the full title of 'Jesus' that '*He is Saviour*'. His calling as the promised deliverer was confirmed by a decisive revelation (Mk. 1:10 f; *cf.* Is.11:2).

As the divine *Lord* He is as well the divine *Saviour*. In other words, He is *Lord* and He is also able to be *Saviour* (*cf.* Acts 2:33-39). For centuries the churches have been reciting in the *Nicene Creed*, 'for us men (human beings) and for our salvation He came down from heaven . . . '.

Lesson 8

Renouncing all that is Evil

At the beginning of the last *Lesson*, we saw that according to the *Order of Confirmation* of the Church of North India, the Bishop asks the candidates to declare their acceptance of Jesus Christ as their *Lord* and *Saviour* and their *commitment* to Him forever. Briefly, we also examined why this was necessary. As we continue to go through the *Order of Confirmation*, we find one of the questions that Bishop asks the candidates is, '*Do you, therefore, renounce all that is evil?*'[28]

Question: What is '*evil*'?

Explanation: In the simplest possible way '*evil*' can be explained as anything that is bad, displeasing and harmful. In other words generally, it means anything that causes pain, unhappiness or misery. Jesus said, '*there is nothing outside man which by going into him can defile him; but the things which come out of a man are what defile him . . . For from within, out of the heart of man, come evil thoughts, fornication, theft, murder, adultery, coveting, wickedness, deceit, licentiousness, envy, slander, pride, foolishness. All these evil things come from within, and they defile a man*' (Mk. 7: 15 & 21-23 RSV). That is why one of the petitions of the prayer that our Lord Himself taught us is, '*but deliver us from evil*' (Mt. 6:13b RSV). In other words, 'save us from

---

[28]*The Book of Worship of the Church of North India (Sec. 15)*, Delhi: ISPCK, 1995, p. 334.

harbouring undesirable evil thoughts'. The Psalmist says, "*For God knows the secrets of the heart*" (Ps. 44:21b RSV).

Question: What is *'sin'*?

Explanation: If we look at all the examples that Jesus mentioned 'which come from within and out of the heart of man or woman', the ultimate cause of them is *self-centeredness*. As a result, either they are against our fellow human beings or God. Thus, anything against the will of God is revolt against His authority and therefore it is *sin*.

In other words, it does happen whenever we put ourselves first. In our day to day life it is generally manifested as 'self-applause, self-assertion, self-advertisement, self indulgence, self-gratification, self-pity, self importance, self-interest and self-will'. The *'self-centeredness'* in fact, is a world-wide phenomenon of human experience'. It is bound to imply an action that injures the covenant between God and His people by disobedience and idolatry. On the contrary, our life should be *God-centered*. Essentially, *'sin'* is directed against God.

Question: Who is the devil?

Explanation: In the Old Testament, it is 'Satan', named as the prince of *evil* (I Chron. 21:1; Zech. 3:1f; Job1-2) – which means 'to make worthless' and bind together both the *evil* deed and its consequences. In the New Testament, it is called as *'devil'* who sinned from the beginning (I Jn. 3:8 *cf.* Mt. 4:1 *ff*) and is considered to be the ruler of the world (Jn. 14:23). He is depicted as hostile to God. But, Jesus came into the world to destroy all his works (I Jn. 3:8). Although his defeat has already been achieved through Jesus' death (Jn. 12:31 & 16:11); he will be totally destroyed by Jesus at the end (Rev. 20:10).

Question: What does it mean by *'denying oneself'*?

Explanation: One of the things that we noticed earlier is *self-centeredness*, which adversely affects our life. If we examine the three temptations of our Lord (Mt. 4:1-11; Mk. 1:12-13 &

Lk. 4:1-13) we would find that in all the three, Jesus was tempted but resisted the temptation to *sin*. He was tempted to assert Himself which He *denied* and did not compromise.

Our Lord also said, *"If any man (or woman) would come after me, let him (her) deny himself (herself) ... "* (Mt. 16:24a RSV).

Arrogance of some kind or other is part of every one of us. Some may be arrogant due to wealth they have acquired; others may be due to their position and status in the society or the amount of academic degrees one holds, etc. It can be also *religious arrogance* – that is *self-righteousness*. Nevertheless, whatever it may be, *arrogance* of any kind makes us *'self-centered'*. We do not care for others. We do not treat them at par with us. Our life should be always *'God-centered'*.

The Psalmist prays:

> 'Create in me a clean heart, O God,
> And put a new and right spirit within me' *(Ps. 51:10 RSV).*

In other words, *'denying oneself'* means, 'controlling of passions, feelings and emotions. It prompts us to be self-sacrificing'. Jesus said, *'Unless a grain of wheat falls into the earth and dies, it remains alone; but if it dies, it bears much fruit'* (Jn. 12:24 RSV). Thus, *'denying oneself'* makes a person to be totally detached from worldly things and to surrender all his or her senses, mind and intellect to God and for the service of others.

Lesson 9

Discipleship
Follower of Jesus Christ

The word *'disciple'* denotes the one who takes another as his or her teacher and model 'to learn' and so means 'learner', 'scholar', 'pupil', etc. In the Old Testament, the word *'disciple'* is used in the Book of Isaiah which means those 'band of followers who would not only preserve the message of the prophet, but make it effective in the days to come' (Is.8:16 RSV).

In the New Testament, the word *'disciple'* is used only in the Gospels and Acts that occurs more than 250 times. Usually, *'the disciples'* seem to mean the small group of those who were continually with Jesus (*cf.* Jn. 13:5, 18:1, 20:19 & 30).

Question: What is Christian Discipleship?

Explanation: It simply means *following* Christ. A true *follower* of Jesus Christ is the one who is personally and decisively committed to Jesus Christ as his or her *Lord* and *Saviour*. Thus, 'the first step is to admit that every individual is a sinner in God's sight and therefore, needs a *Saviour* from our sins'.

Question: But, what does *following* Christ means?

Explanation: Although 'it is not always easy to determine whether Jesus Christ's *'disciples'* means a small group living in close fellowship with Him or the larger body of those who accepted Him as their teacher or their leader; Jesus repeatedly said, *"Follow Me"*. Thus, the choice is of Jesus, not the *disciples* (Mk. 3:19). Jesus expects His *disciples* to renounce everything else (Mt.10:38*f.*). To be His *disciples* is not a stepping stone toward a promising career. He is not only their Teacher but also their *Lord* (Mt.10:24). Since, Master is also Servant (Mk.10:45), servanthood also involves suffering as also for the *followers* of Jesus. As a matter of fact, Jesus gave three lessons on *'discipleship'* to His disciples (Mk. 8:34-38, 9:33-37 & 10:35-45). Same are applicable to all of us who claim to be His *followers*.

Jesus told his *disciples*, 'He must suffer before He reigns' (Mk. 8:31-33 *cf.* 9:30-32 & 10:32-34) and, hence, *"If any man (or Woman) would come after me, let him (or her) deny himself (or herself) and take up his (or her) cross and follow me"* (Mt. 16:24; Mk. 8:34 ff. RSV). His *followers* must also walk the same path. Since God's values are not the same as those of human beings and if we do things according to God's will, we are bound to find ourselves in conflict with the world's ideals. Thus, *following* Christ demands a total *commitment* to Him and selfless service for others.

In fact, 'several of Christ's first disciples literally had to take up the cross and die a martyr's death. Today, Christ calls us to various other forms of sacrifice – such as, some are called to abandon their wealth, reputation, friends and relatives, country and even their life. Others have to bear the unspectacular but unrelenting burdens of their family, their work and their communities. However, without sacrifice we cannot serve God nor find true fulfillment'.

When Jesus told His disciples; He, in fact asked them to count the cost of *following* Him. Let us then put it this way as to what does it cost us to *follow* Christ; *'Following'* Jesus Christ demands two pre-conditions: First, *"to deny oneself"* and secondly, *"to take up ones cross."*

Jesus also rejects exclusiveness of every kind – such as based on class, caste or race and as well as financial distinction.

The fundamental idea seems to be: get rid of differences which *alienate* one from another and thus, get rid of envy, hatred, malice and all uncharitableness. In the Gospel according to St. Luke, chapter 14, there is a call for renunciation (vv.26-27), counting the cost (vv 28-32), and drastic sacrifice (vs. 33) - even at the cost of one's home, business and possession (Mk. 10:21).

Question: What is the similarity between the *'band of the followers'* of prophet Isaiah and the *'disciples'* of Jesus?

Explanation: To *follow* Jesus, does not mean merely passing on His teachings or becoming the faithful custodians of His insights, but to be His *"witnesses"* (Acts 1:8). Thus, to be Jesus Christ's faithful *disciple* one has to be *'God-centered'* and discard all kinds of *arrogance* from our life that amounts to *'self-centeredness'*.

IV. Christian 'Sadhna': Spiritual Discipline

44

Lesson 10

The Ten Commandments
Called to be Holy

Generally, the word *'Discipline'* means training – 'especially of the kind that produces self-control, orderliness, obedience and capacity for co-operation'. In Hindi, the word *'sadhna'*, although, literally denotes 'means'; it is also translated as *'spiritual discipline'*.

Question: What do we mean by *'Spiritual Discipline'*?

Explanation: In the Old Testament, the word *'holy'* suggests the separation of a person or thing for a divine use – that is, 'to set apart' for God's purpose rather than any ethical purity. The New Testament emphasizes the ethical nature of *'holiness'* and presents it as the supreme goal of Christian living; it also emphasizes the eternal permanence of moral character (Rev. 22:11).

Saint Peter says, 'as *obedient children, do not be conformed to the passions of your former ignorance, but as he who called you is holy, be holy yourselves in all your conduct; since it is written, "You shall be holy, for I am holy"'* (I Pet. 1:14-16 *cf.* Lev.11:44-45 RSV). Saint Paul also says, you are *'called to be saints'* (Rom. 1:7 RSV). But, the *'holiness'* does not suggest projecting a false image of pious folk with long faces. Instead, true *'holiness'* is a *'Christ-likeness'*. Jesus said, *'As the Father has sent me, even so, I send you'* (Jn. 20:21 RSV).

Question: What is the basic standard for *'Holy Living'*?

Explanation: The *Ten Commandments* (Ex. 20:2-17 & Deut. 5:6-21) are still considered the basic standard for *Holy Living*. They are known as the Laws of Moses and in fact, God's Laws. They guide us as how to live a life that is pleasing to God. They can be clubbed into two groups: *'Our duty to God'* and *'Our duty to fellow human beings'*. The first five commandments concern our duty to God:

1. *'You shall have no other gods before me'*: This is what God demands as our exclusive worship. He should be first in our life;

2. *'You shall not make yourself a graven image . . .'* : If the first commandment requires our exclusive worship, the second demands that it shall be spiritual. Jesus said, "God is spirit, and those who worship him must worship him in spirit" (Jn. 4:24a RSV).

3. *'You shall not take the name of the Lord your God in vain'*: We should avoid swearing in God's name and taking His name in vain by our hypocrisies. We call God in our prayers but contradict it in our daily living.

4. *'Remember the sabbath day, to keep it holy'*: Sunday is "the Lord's Day', and not our day. Jesus said, "The Sabbath was made for men" (Mk. 2:27a). To attend Sunday worship is our duty. It is a must and, we must also give proper rest to our body and mind. In other words, they should not take each other's place. We must take note of the change in observance of Sabbath from the seventh day to the first day of the week as 'the Lord's Day' to commemorate the Resurrection of our Lord (Mt. 28:1-6; Mk. 16:1-6; Lk. 1-5 & Jn. 20:1-18).

5. *'Honour your father and your mother'*: This commandment belongs to the first group of the law – that is *our duty to God* – as 'They represent to us God's authority, in fact all elders. Our behaviour towards all elders and parents often betrays our real attitude towards God'. *'This is*

the first commandment with a promise' (*cf.* Eph. 6:2 RSV).

The next five commandments deal with our duty to our fellow human beings. Our duty to our fellow human beings is summed up by our Lord in the golden rule, "*So whatever you wish that men would do to you, do so to them; for this is the law and the prophets*" (Mt. 7:12 RSV). Saint Paul says, "*Love does no wrong to a neighbour; therefore love is the fulfilling of the law*" (Rom. 13:8-10 RSV). In other words, if we truly love other persons, we shall respect their rights and desire their good. These remaining commandments enumerate five offences against love. They are:

6. '*You shall not kill*': To take a person's life, the most precious possession, is the first and greatest denial of love. Jesus said that, even being angry and using cruel or bad words or losing our temper and hating other people in our hearts is as bad as committing murder (Mt. 5:21-22).

7. '*You shall not commit adultery*': Adultery is sexual intercourse between *married* people, other than one's husband or wife. Sex is God's precious gift and, hence, is to be used and enjoyed in its proper place and time, which is only in marriage. We must also remember that our body is the temple of God in which the Holy Spirit dwells (I Cor. 3:16-17).

8. '*You shall not steal*': It includes all dishonesty and cheating.

9. '*You shall not bear false witness*': A *follower* of Jesus is expected to be honest both in word as well as in deed (Ps. 141:3; Jas. 1:26 & 3:1-12).

10. '*You shall not covet*': Saint Paul says, "*Covetousness is idolatry*" (Eph. 5:5 RSV). It is a sin not only against someone but also one's own self. A follower of Jesus has to be content with what God has given him or her.

The Ten Commandments are mostly negative – such as: "*thou shall not*" – Jesus, however, summarized the teaching of these Ten Commandments by the supreme law of 'love', which is positive. The biblical understanding of 'love' is the desire to give and to enrich – "*For God so loved the world that he gave his only Son*" (Jn. 3:16a RSV). The Ten Commandments show us as to how this principle has to operate in practice.

Lesson 11

The Holy Bible
The Word of God

Every religion has its Sacred Book(s) – such as; *Bhagavad-Gita* (Hinduism), *Holy Quran* (Islam), *Granth Saheb* (Sikhism), etc. So also Christianity has *the Holy Bible.*

The word *bible* comes from the Greek word, *biblos,* originally means 'book'. But the Bible or the book that we are talking about is known as *'The Holy Bible';* as distinguished from other sacred writings.

Question: What is the *Holy Bible*?

Explanation: The Holy Bible contains 66 books and these books are grouped into two parts – that is: The Old Testament and The New Testament. The word *testament* means 'covenant' or 'promise'. The 39 books of the Old Testament were written before the time of Jesus. These books are associated with the old 'covenant' between God and man which means human beings (Ex. 24: 7 *ff.*) and look forward to a new 'covenant' (Jer. 31:31 *ff.*), which is the New Testament as inaugurated by Christ (I Cor. 11:25 & Heb. 8:13).

The 39 books in the Old Testament are arranged in three divisions: i) *The Law*: (Genesis, Exodus, Leviticus, Numbers and Deuteronomy), also known as Pentateuch; ii) *The Prophets*: (Joshua, Judges, Samuel, Kings, Isaiah, Jeremiah, Ezekiel,

Hosea, Joel, Amos, Obadiah, Jonah, Micah, Nahum, Habakkuk, Zephaniah, Haggai, Zechariah and Malachi); and iii) *The Writings*: (The Psalms, Proverbs, Job, Daniel, Ezra, Nehemiah, Chronicles, the Song of Songs, Ruth, Lamentation, Ecclesiastes and Esther).

There are 27 books in the New Testament which also can be divided into four divisions: The Gospels (four); the Acts of the Apostles (one); Letters written by apostles and 'apostolic men' (twenty-one); and Revelation.

Question: Who wrote *the Holy Bible*?

Explanation: The answer is simple. Each book of *the Bible* has at least two authors: God and a human author and sometimes even two or more human authors.

Question: Thus the pertinent question is, 'If God and human beings wrote *the Bible*, then what part was God's and what part belongs to the human author (s)?'

Explanation: The answer could be that God used human beings as His instruments. For example, when we write a letter, in any language, we use a pen as our instrument for writing. Then, shall we say that it is the pen that writes? No! In fact, we write the letter. On the other hand, the letter is written by a pen. Likewise, God used human beings. But, we must not forget that there is a vast difference between a human being and a pen. Human beings have feelings, prejudices, ways of thinking that depends on his/her education and circumstances. All these affect the written work just as the flatness or roundness of the nib of our pen affects our writing. For example, Jeremiah was an angry and moody man; David was a poet; Paul was a fiery man of action; and Luke was a historian. God used all of them as writing instruments according to their nature. God is above and behind and controlling everything. Therefore, each word in *the Bible* is due to Him as much as to His 'writing instruments' – that is, human authors (Jer. 1:5-9 *cf.* Is. 6:8ff; Ezk. 2 & II Pet. 1:21).

In other words, God unveiled (*revealed*) that which He desired human beings to know some spiritual truth and quickened (*inspired*) the mind and soul to perceive and understand what had been unveiled. *"The heavens are telling the glory of God ..."* (Ps. 19:1-4).

Question: When were the books of the New Testament written?

Explanation: Jesus did not write anything about Himself or His teachings. Instead, He left a deep impression of Himself and His teachings on the heart and mind of those who not only had the privilege of knowing Him closely but also, loved Him. Their main qualification was that in their own way they were the *'followers'* and so the *'disciples'* of Jesus Christ and initially the members of the group, which later was recognised as the church. Therefore, we must remember that the church existed much before the books of the New Testament were written.

Later, some of these *'followers'* and *'disciples'* of Jesus wrote books about His life and teaching; obviously, then 'these books were written by members of the church to members of the church'. They were individuals with different backgrounds and experiences. Each one of them had a different personality. For example, the four Gospels differ from one another in many ways. Therefore, we find four distinct pictures of Jesus as presented in these Gospels.

Question: What is the main message that runs through the pages of the Bible?

Explanation: The central message is the story of *salvation*. In other words, the story of the Bible begins with Divine initiative of *reconciliation* (Gen. 3:9) and 'finally, God spoke in His Son – summing up, confirming and transcending the earlier revelation – conveyed in many ways (Heb. 1:1f)'.

That is why, with all their differences, the writers of the four Gospels had one common message to communicate, as

Saint John the writer of the fourth Gospel says, *"For God so loved the world that he gave his only Son, that whoever believes in him should not perish but have eternal life. For God sent the Son into the world, not to condemn the world, but that the world might be saved through him"* (Jn. 3:16-17 RSV).

Thus, 'The great theme of the Bible is the action of God seeking in love to realize His holy will in communion with man' (i.e. human being).' It is the hope that is set before us (*Ref*. Lk. 21:33).

In the Bible God teaches us to see Him behind all human events. In other words, behind the human agents with their personal intentions, faith in God is revealed, such as Joseph's brothers were God's instruments (Gen. 45:4-15). In the story of Saul there is God's plan (I Sam. 9:15-10:1). Cyrus also turned to be an instrument in God's hands (Is. 45:1-13) and so also Caesar Augustus became God's instrument (Lk. 2:1-14).

Question: Why do we usually call '*The Bible*' as '*The Holy Bible*'?

Explanation: Since God is completely remote from human beings, He should be feared, pleased, obeyed and worshipped. Thus, anything that is also connected with religion must be set apart as *holy*. *The Bible* or the book that we are talking about is known '*The Holy Bible*'; as it is the *Book of Holiness* and therefore, it is different from other books. That is why we consider it '*holy*'. The words *holy, holiness, sacred, saint*, indicate some form of separateness, consecration or uniqueness. This idea of '*separateness*' is found in almost all the ancient religions and in the earliest forms of faith.

Question: What is the difference between *the Bible* and *the Scripture(s)*?

Explanation: The word '*scripture(s)*' in the New Testament broadly refers to what we now call the Old Testament, in which the gospel is rooted and which Christ fulfilled (Lk. 24:44; II Tim.3:15*ff*).

Question: Why is *The Holy Bible* also called the *'word of God'*?

Explanation: As has already been mentioned earlier, every religion has its Sacred Book(s) – such as; *Bhagavad Gita* (Hinduism), *Holy Quran* (Islam), *Granth Saheb* (Sikhism), etc. – *the Holy Bible,* is unique as it is also considered *the 'word of God'*.

In the Old Testament, *'the word of God'* is a phrase used 394 times of a divine communication in one of several forms. It is considered as an extension of God's personality and hence is to be heeded by all (Ps. 103:20). It stands forever (Is. 40:8) and once uttered cannot return unfulfilled (Is.55:11). It means simply any communication made by God to human beings – especially through a prophet. In the book of Jeremiah the phrase *'the word of the Lord'* occurs more than 50 times. In the New Testament it is used for the Christian message (Mk. 2:2 & Gal. 6:6).

In the Gospel according to John (Jn. 1:1), the concept of the *'word'* occurs most explicitly signifying Christ as the *'the Word'*, in Greek *Logos,* - the incarnate Word – which in New Testament occurs more than 300 times.

Normally, there are three kinds of 'word', spoken, written and lived. When we speak, our *spoken* word cannot be seen or touched, but it makes its impact, which is real. When we write, our *written* word cannot be withdrawn or pulled back. We cannot deny it. Therefore, it has to be used with great care. Whereas, the word lived is human personality - that is, the way we present ourselves to others. *The Holy Bible* is all three in the Person of Jesus Christ: His words, spoken, recorded and lived out.

The Holy Bible is the written 'word of God' because through it we find Jesus Christ. In other words:

i) *The Bible* is the 'word of God', because it is the place where the broken relationship between humans and God is repaired.

ii) *The Bible* is the 'word of God', because it was written by men who knew God, as they loved and obeyed Him.

iii) *The Bible* is the 'word of God', because it tells of the self revealing and saving acts of God culminating in the life events of Jesus Christ.

iv) *The Bible* is the 'word of God', because in it alone we are confronted with the life and teaching of Jesus Christ.

Thus, the Bible is Divine. As, this is God's word to human beings: "*Thus says the Lord*" (Jer. 9:23; 51:1; Ezk. 30:6, 10 & 13 and *cf.* 1:1; Is. 1:2; and Jer. 1:4). So also Jesus said, "And there will be signs in sun and moon and stars, and upon the earth ... then they will see the Son of man coming in a cloud with power and great glory ... Heaven and earth will pass away, but my words will not pass away"(Lk.21:25-33).

Question: What is the position of *the Holy Bible* in the Church of North India?

Explanation: "It accepts the Holy Scriptures of the Old and the New Testament as the inspired Word of God containing all things necessary for salvation, and as the supreme and decisive standard of faith, and acknowledges that the church must always be ready to correct and reform itself in accordance with the teaching of those Scriptures as the Holy Spirit shall reveal it."[29]

---

[29] The Constitution of the Church of North India and Bye-Laws (as amended up to 21st October, 2005), *Part I, Chapter I, Section III, Clause 2.* p. 4.

Lesson 12

The Lord's Prayer
Prayer and Worship

It is only God's grace or His power that can sanctify us and there are various ways through which His strength can reach us. These are called *"the means of grace"* because they are channels through which God's power can come to us. They are: Prayer, the Holy Bible and the Holy Communion. Of course, there are others also such as Christian Worship and Christian Fellowship.

When we go through the pages of the four Gospels we find that our Lord was a *'man of prayer'*. Constantly, it was in prayer that He was in communication with his Father. Thus, if that was so important for Jesus, then what about us?

If we want to build up our spiritual strength, then all the time we need to discipline our Christian life by taking full advantage of these *"means of grace"*. In order to grow spiritually and make steady progress in our life as a *follower* of Jesus Christ, there is nothing more important than spending some "quiet times" with God in prayer.

Question: What is Prayer?

Explanation: If we truly believe that God is there eternally, *'prayer'* also has to be there. Because *'prayer'* is human's instinctive tendency, it must be incorporated into the very constitution of human nature. It lies in our hearts which God has made for *fellowship* with Himself (Ex. 6:28; Deut. 12:9; I Cor. 16:18; II Cor. 7:13; I Pet. 4:14; Heb. 3:7-4:11).

Thus in the simplest possible way, *'prayer'* can be defined as being sensitive to be in *fellowship* of the Heavenly Father and also to *converse* with Him as one speaking in a natural way to his or her human father. Jesus revealed that God our 'Heavenly Father knows all our needs and provides for them' (Mt. 6:23-25); 'He listens to our every *prayer*' (Mt. 7:7-11; 18:19-20); 'He is full of compassion towards everyone' (Lk. 6:36); 'He is generous in forgiving our sins' (Mt. 18:27); and 'He defends us from danger' (Mt. 10:28-31).

Traditionally, *'prayer'* can be classified and also defined as adoration, thanksgiving, confession, intercession and Petitions. However, such modes of *'prayer'* are vocal. *'Prayer'* can also be classified as meditation or contemplation which is talking within the inner most being of the believer. As a matter of fact, this kind of prayer is simply to realize God's presence in a special way.

Question: What is *'Prayer of Silence'* or importance of being *'Silent in Prayer'*?

Explanation: The Psalmist says, *'Be still, and know that I am God'* (Ps. 46:10a RSV). We all come across the experience of such moments in our life when the words or any action fails to express our intimate relationship with our dear ones. It is then, SILENCE only can communicate in its best and deepest sense. Today, we live in a noise-polluted world. It is almost, impossible to be able to have actual physical *silence*. Even, two-thousand years ago, precisely because of such difficulties our Lord told His disciples to cultivate a still centre *inside themselves*. He said, *'when you pray, go into your room and shut the door and pray to your Father Who is in secret'* (Mt. 6:6a RSV). Jesus must have been speaking not of a secret place but of that 'portable sanctuary inside our heart' which we carry around with us and to which we can withdraw at any time and place. Saint

Paul said, *'Do you not know that you are God's temple and that God's Spirit dwells in you?'* (I Cor. 3:16 RSV). Thus, our bodies should be houses of *prayer* and our life a life of *prayer*. *'Prayer'* is as essential to our inner life as breath is to our body.

There is a beautiful story about Jesus and His disciples recorded in the Gospel according to Saint Luke: *'He was praying in a certain place and when he ceased, one of His disciples said to Him,* **"Lord, teach us to pray"***'* (Lk. 11:1a RSV).

Question: Shall we assume that Jesus' disciples had never prayed earlier?

Explanation: No! probably all of them must have been men of *'prayer'*. They were devout Jews. It seems as though they must have felt some difference between Jesus' prayers and their own. That is why Jesus had been praying with them and when finished, the disciples requested Him *'Lord, teach us to pray'*.

Question: What is that *Prayer* Jesus Himself taught to His disciples?

Explanation: After the Pentecost (Acts 2:1-4), more and more people became the *followers* of Jesus Christ; the apostles taught the *prayer* to these *followers* that Jesus Himself had taught them. In fact, it became customary for the *prayer* to be taught to catechumens as part of preparation for their baptism.

First of all, Jesus taught the most comprehensive lesson about His Father's love for us – human beings – as contained in the words, *Our Father*. It begins with our relationship to God and to one another in God, not 'my God' but *'our Father*. As we pray, our intimate relation with our Father is renewed. Can we imagine anything in us that does not come from Him?

It is *'The Lord's Prayer'*, the prayer that He Himself used, adapted to our needs and taught to His Disciples (Mt. 6:9-13 & Lk. 11:2-4). It is a prayer which is all embracing and covering all our spiritual and material wellbeing and nothing has been omitted from it.

The body of the prayer falls into two main parts. The first contains three petitions concerning the glory of God: the hallowing His Name; the final coming of His Kingdom; and the fulfillment of His will on earth and heaven. The second part contains the personal needs of His disciples – such as provision, pardon and protection. Let us see briefly as to what they mean to us:

"Hallowed be thy name": The name is power. It can only be invoked with faith, love and trust in the One whose whole being is embraced in it. The psalmist sings in Praise to the Lord; *"O sing to the Lord a new song, for he has done marvellous things!"* (Ps. 98:1a RSV). The Prophet Isaiah acclaims his faith in the name, *"O Lord, thou art my God; I will exalt thee, I will praise thy name; for thou hast done wonderful things . . . "* (Is. 25:1 RSV). David did so quite literally when he faced Goliath: *'You come to me with a sword and with a spear and with a javelin; but I come to you* **in the name of the Lord of hosts** *. . . this day the Lord will deliver you into my hand . . .'* (I Sam. 17: 45-46 RSV). The name is power but not something filled with magic.

"Thy kingdom come": To pray this prayer, is to further the process of the final transformation of all things – that is: human society – which also includes our own lives. Thus, this petition concerns something yet to be achieved.

"Thy will be done": We can say, *'Your will be done'* with ease and relative comfort. But, when we are caught up in a situation where His will conflicts with our hopes, desires, ambitions and longings, then it does not become a comfortable prayer but a cry of anguish. This tests our love for God as this prayer poses a challenge for us.

"Give us today our daily bread": 'Bread' is usually taken to cover the basic necessities of life – i.e., food, shelter, clothing, health, etc. – *'Give us'* means that the 'bread' is a gift from God to be received to share. *'Daily bread'*, of course is a necessity but should not be treated as a luxury. In fact, 'bread' is the

most universal symbol of unity. It is a sign of fellowship and a bond of friendship.

"And forgive our sins . . . ": We all need the healing and wholeness that comes from forgiveness. *The Lord's Prayer*, however, reminds us that forgiveness cannot be earned or deserved. It is free and received out of God's kindness.

" . . . as we forgive those who sin against us": Although 'forgiveness' is free and we get it out of kindness, there are always conditions. The whole tenor of Jesus' teaching bears out the principle of forgiving freely – not nursing grudges, nor harbouring anger or resentment (Mt. 5:22 *cf.* Mk. 11:25; Mt. 5:38-42; Eph. 4:32). Jesus said, '*I say to you, Love your enemies and pray for those who persecute you . . . You, therefore, must be perfect . . .*' (Mt. 5:44 & 48 RSV).

"Lead us not into temptation, but deliver us from evil": This can be a prayer to be saved from making a mistake through hardness of heart.

Thus the Lord's Prayer is a model prayer which summarizes the teaching of Jesus about God's Kingdom and serves as a pattern for all prayer. On this pattern our life of prayer must be based'. *The Lord's Prayer* begins with '*Our Father . . .*' and ends with '*Thine is the kingdom . . .*' (Mt. 6:13b RSV). Our Father is a King and therefore, why should not we offer Him praise?

When we go through the pages of the Bible we come across several places where references are made about *'worship'* (Gen. 22:5; Deut. 12:31; I Chron. 16:31; Ps. 95:6; Mt. 2:2 & 4:10; Jn. 4:22; Acts 17:23; and Rev. 4:10). In fact, its form may differ but it is something that is common to all the faiths.

Question: What is *Worship*?

Explanation: The word *'worship'* comes from an old English word 'worthship' – giving to God His true worth as Creator, Redeemer, and indwelling Spirit. Thus, *'worship'* is human response to these divine activities. In the Book of Revelation a scene of Heavenly Worship is narrated as: *'Worthy art thou, our Lord and God, to receive glory and honour and power, for thou didst create all things, and by Thy will they existed and were created'* (Rev. 4:11 RSV).

The Psalmist says, *'O come, let us worship and bow down, let us kneel before the Lord, our Maker!'* (Ps.95:6 RSV). *'Worship'* is the most unselfish form of prayer because we worship God for what He is and not for what we can get out of Him. It is our duty that we owe to Him Who is continually creating, sustaining and holding us in His being (Ps. 104; Is. 40:12-31; Job 36:24-37 & 38:1-42:6). He is great and Holy (Ps. 19:9; 34:9 & 11; Prov. 9:10 & 14:26-27; Is. 11:2-3 & Acts 9:31). Above all, *'God is love'* revealed to us in and through His only Son Jesus Christ (Jn. 3:16-17; Gal. 2:20). It is human response to God's initiative; *'we love, because He first loved us'* (I Jn. 4:19 RSV). However, since it is human response, it must be with a higher level of reverence (*shradha*) and devotion (*bhakti*).

As far as bowing, kneeling and lying at His feet is concerned that is personal expression of our love for Him and varies with every individual and must be spontaneous.

V. Christian Fellowship

Lesson 13

The Church

The Bishop asks the candidates, 'Will you follow Jesus Christ in the *fellowship of His Church?*' In our *Lessons* on '*Christian Commitment*', we have already dealt with the subject of '*Following Jesus Christ*' under 'Discipleship'.

Question: What is the *Church*?

Explanation: We have learned earlier that we were initiated as members of the *Church* through our baptism. This English word '*church*' comes from a Greek word *ekklesia*, which means 'called out'.

In the New Testament '*church*' is also used as meaning 'a local assembly of people'.

According to Saint Matthew (Mt. 16:18), it clearly refers to the future Christian community and not a building. Saint Paul however calls the Christian community as the '*Body of Christ*' (I Cor. 12:12-27; Rom. 12:5f; Eph. 1:23) and '*Christ being its Head*' (Eph. 1:22 & 5:23; Col. 1:18 & 24 & 2:19). But the essence of the '*Church*' is that it is a 'called' society and not an organization devised and set up by human beings, it is a congregation called out by God.

It is said that 'Christianity is essentially a 'social' religion'.

Question: In the Creeds, the *Church* is described as *One, Holy, Catholic* and *Apostolic*. What do these words mean?

Explanation: It means that the *Church* is '*One*'; because Christ is one, and the *Church* is His body (I Jn. 4:2 *ff*). It is built upon the one Lord Jesus and is so closely associated with Him that it is called His Body. This can be explained this way also; as there is one Christ, so He has one *Church*. In other words, the 'oneness' of the *Church* is primarily the sharing of one life, that is the life of Christ. So also, the object of its existence is the bringing of all human beings into the 'oneness' of God in accordance with our Lord's High Priestly Prayer, '*that they may be one, even as we are one*' (Jn. 17:22). Every repetition of the Creed should come as a shock to our Christian conscience. The *Church* is '*One*'.

Holiness is the peculiar quality that is associated with God (I Sam. 2:2). Although, the *Church* – the community of the called out by God – as yet is far from '*holy*'; we believe in the 'holiness of the Church'. The *Church* is '*Holy*' because the Holy Spirit dwells in it and sanctifies its members. It is set apart in Christ (I Pet. 1:15-16 & 2:5-9) and separated for God. 'The idea of separation from the rest of humankind and being set apart for God's use was written into the very name of this new worldwide community. The word that Jesus chose for it was "*church*". It has already been mentioned that in Greek it is *ekklesia*, which means 'called out". But, it does not mean that God has called His people to withdraw from the world. They are to be in the world but not of it, like salt in food and light in the world (Mt.5:13 & 14). The test therefore, by which any group of Christians is recognized as a part of the '*Holy*' church is not if it contains sinners or not, but whether it is really doing the work of turning those sinners into saints.

The third word for the *Church* that is used in the Creeds is that, it is '*Catholic*'. The root of the word is from Greek, which sometimes is translated as 'universal'. Of course, it certainly gives part of the meaning, for the *Catholic* Church is the church which is the home of all nations and intends to reach '*to the end of the earth*' (Acts 1:8). It takes in every nation and kindred and people and tongues (Rev. 7:9). But in reality, the word '*catholic*' carries with it the sense of *'altogether-ness'*. The *Church* not only embraces all human beings but teaches the whole truth with due balance and proportion.

The fourth and last word used to describe the *Church* is *'apostolic'*. The word 'apostle' means 'sent'. Jesus was the Apostle of the Father (Heb. 3:1), and in His turn He chose and sent out those whom He called 'Apostles telling them, *"As the Father hast sent me, even so I send you"* (Jn. 20:21b RSV). We notice that the Creed does not mention the 'Apostles', but only the *apostolic* Church. Thus, the emphasis is on the whole *Church* – the community of the called out by God – as *apostolic* and missionary. The *Church* exists to carry on the work for which the apostles were sent out, continues steadfastly in the Apostles' teaching and fellowship, and also to preach the Gospel to the whole world. As far as the *Church* is faithful in her mission, she is apostolic in her aim, her teaching and her ministry; She fails to be apostolic when she ceases to represent Christ. Jesus said, *"You shall be my witnesses . . . to the end of the earth"* (Acts 1:8).

The Apostles' Creed also introduces under the clause concerning the Holy Spirit certain points connected with the *Church* – such as The Holy Spirit as the indweller of the *Church* (I Cor. 3:16); Local *Church* as the church in Jerusalem (Acts 8:1, 15:4); in Antioch (Acts 8:1); in Corinth (I Cor. 1:2); a group of churches (Acts 9:31 & 15:41); the *Church* universal (Eph. 5:25-29); and the *Church's* ministry (Eph. 4:11-16) for preaching the Word, leading in Public Worship and administration of discipline and the *Church's* authority to legislate its life and order (Mt.18:15-20, I Cor. 5:9-13); as well as our duty to work and suffer for His Body the *Church,* as Saint Paul did (Col. 1:24).

Ultimately, the *Church* is to be the community which embodies the Spirit of Christ and carries on His loving, serving and saving work.

Lesson 14

Privileges and Duties

In the previous *Lesson* we looked into the biblical understanding of the meaning of *'Church'*. But, the question the Bishop asks is. *'Will you follow Jesus Christ in the fellowship of His church?'*

Question: What does *the fellowship of His Church* mean'?

Explanation: Can we imagine a human being living from birth without any contact with any other fellow human being? As a matter of fact, human personality cannot develop in isolation; nor human society can function without understanding, communication and cooperation between people. We function only through relationship with others.

Christianity is a social religion. Christian life is not to be lived in splendid isolation. *Christian Fellowship* is a family in which we are all brothers and sisters in Christ. Jesus, therefore taught us to pray: "*Our Father . . .* "(Mt. 6:9). For God's purpose is not to save independent souls but to build a *Church* - a community of His followers as a *'Witnessing Community'* (Acts 1:8). Saint Paul said, *'For just as the body is one and has many members of the body, so it is with Christ'* (I Cor. 12:12 RSV). This is what *'Christian Fellowship'* means.

However, we also know that, people do not enter the Kingdom of God as congregations but as individuals.

Through *Confirmation* we become Communicant Members of the Church - in this case, the Church of North India. Consequently, a *Christian Fellowship* offers *privileges* to its members as well as demands from them certain *duties* to be fulfilled.

Question: What are my *privileges* in *Christian Fellowship*?

Explanation: We must fully enjoy and get the maximum benefits and *privileges* of membership of *Christian Fellowship* for our spiritual growth.

a) We receive the life which the Spirit gives and which amounts to *being born again*; as Saint Paul puts it in his letter to the Christians in Galatia, "*a new creation*" (Gal. 6:15 *cf.* Jn. 3:5).

b) We become God's children, the Life in Spirit (Rom. 8:16). 'The Presbyter, having blessed the water, pours it on the child's head "*in the name of the Father, and of the Son, and of the Holy Spirit.*" At this moment the child is "*born again*" – born through water and the Holy Spirit. Shortly afterwards, the Presbyter gives thanks to God for making the child His own child by adoption'.[30]

c) We are initiated into the *Fellowship of the Church*, the Body of Christ. 'At every baptism, Jesus Christ, using the hands of a human being is Himself the baptiser. He receives the child and makes him/her a member of His Body, the church. Just as a new shoot is grafted into a fruit tree, so also through baptism we are grafted into Christ. And as the life of the tree flows into the shoot, so Christ gives His life to the baptized child. Thus the great blessing which is given in baptism is nothing less than a share in the life of Christ'[31] Himself.

---

[30] *A Pastor's Handbook for the Church of North India*, Delhi: ISPCK, 1983, p. 9.

[31] *Ibid.*, p. 9.

d) 'The privilege of participating in the government of His church'.[32]

For some, attending Sunday Worship is the only thing that they could think of to make their participation in *Christian Fellowship*; whereas, there are several other things where they should lend their support as part of their *Christian duty*.

Question: What are my bounden *duties* as a member of the church?

Explanation: As we claim that the church is the Body of Christ – a community of His followers – our first and foremost duty is to live up to its *'witness'* by upholding its own ideals. Secondly, we truly present ourselves as an alternative society which eclipses the values and standards of the world. Our duty above all is to work and suffer, if need be, for His Body – the church – as Saint Paul did (Col. 1:24).

Question: What about the *Christian Fellowship* in the Holy Communion?

Explanation: **The Holy Communion** is the central service of the church instituted by the Lord Jesus Himself and observed by the earliest Christians (Acts 2:42 & 46). It is Saint Paul's expression (I Cor. 11:20). It is described as the fellowship meal of Christians by invitation of the Lord Jesus. Five times in ICorinthians 11, in a space of eighteen verses, Saint Paul uses the verb "*to come together*". Thus, the *Lord's Supper* is a gathering together of Christian people where Jesus Christ Himself objectively and really is present to make Himself known in our hearts by faith. Then, we too can have the privilege of having an experience like Jacob, 'surely the Lord is in this place' (Gen.28:16 RSV). As a result then, we can also *'witness'* to others (non-believers) who too may declare, '*God is really among you*' (*cf.* I Cor. 14:24-25 RSV).

---

[32] *CNI Constitution, Part I, Chapter I, Section 5, Sub-Section A, Clause 13.*

Lesson 15

Vocation and Ministry

The Latin word *'Vocation'* means a 'Person's sense of being *called* for a task, the occupation or *calling* that one follows'. In English, its equivalent is *'calling'*.

God has a purpose for the lives of His people. Saint Paul says, *'We are His workmanship, created in Christ Jesus for good works, which God prepared beforehand'* (Eph. 2:10). If that is so, then as *followers* of Jesus Christ it is our duty to find out as to what is God's purpose for our lives? – In other words, 'what is my *Vocation*?' or 'what is my *Ministry*?'

Question: What is the biblical understanding of *'Vocation'*?

Explanation: The first and foremost thing is to remember that it is God who *'calls'* us. Therefore, its emphasis is not on what we as human beings do, but on what God has *called* us to do.

In the New Testament, the verb to *'call'* occurs about 150 times, and most cases are of God *calling* human beings. In the Old Testament, we see God *called* Moses (Ex. 3:1-4:17), Samuel (I Sam. 3:1-2) and the prophets (*e.g.* Is. 6: 1-8). In the New Testament Jesus *called* the Twelve (Mk. 3:13-19) and later Saul of Tarsus (Acts 9:1-6).

Question: According to the Scriptures what does God *call* us to do?

Explanation: In a general sense, God *calls* all of us to be something rather than to do anything special – such as the followers of Jesus Christ in Corinth were "*called to be saints*" (I Cor. 2:24 *cf.* Rom. 1:7a, Eph. 1:1a, Phil. 1:1a & Col. 2:1a). We are *called* to 'holiness' (I Cor. !:2). Since God Himself is Holy, He calls us also to be *holy* (I Pet. 1:15; I Thess. 4:7; II Tim. 1:9). We find Jesus asking people just to *follow* Him which means first 'to be His disciples' (I Pet. 3:9). In reality, He demands from us '*Christ-likeness*'. He said to His disciples, "*As the Father has sent me, even so I send you*" (Jn. 20:21).

We must never overlook the most important aspect of our *calling* as being His followers. When Jesus *called* His twelve disciples, the first of the three purposes was '*to be with Him*' (Mk. 3:14). God has *called* us '*into the fellowship of His Son Jesus Christ our Lord*' (I Cor. 1:9). Thus as members of one body we are called to peace (Col. 3:15) – that is reconciliation with each other – in the *fellowship* with Jesus Christ as we belong not only to Christ but also to one another.

Since, God is interested in the whole of life there has to be no difference between the calling of those who are ordained and those who are serving in secular jobs, married men and women, as whose life too is consecrated to their respective responsibilities. To be precise, it means that the whole of our life belongs to God and is part of His *calling*.

For most of us it seems that God whom we worship and adore, is confined only to religious buildings, sacred books, religious rites and rituals. This is not true. He is the Lord of the whole of our life – whether we are in the church or at work, school or college, home or market, playing or travelling. – We must remember that our *Vocation* covers all areas of our life and its activities.

Question: What is the biblical understanding of *'Ministry'*?

Explanation: The New Testament term for *Ministry* is 'service', from which comes the word 'deacon'. The pattern for *Christian Ministry* is supplied by Jesus, 'who came not to be served but to serve' (Mk. 10:45). Service done to others is also reckoned to be done to Christ (Mt. 25:44) – such service is a gift of God (Col. 4:17 *cf.* Rom. 12:7). In fact, *Christian Ministry* derives its essential nature directly from the person and work of Christ. In other words, the greatness of a community of His disciples is to be measured in terms of willingness to *serve*. Subsequently in Christian community any position, office or work is essentially a *'Ministry'*, a *service* to God and to fellow members. Thus, the exercise of the apostolic commission is a *'ministry'* (*cf.* Rom. 11:13; II Cor. 6:3 *ff.* & Acts 20:24).

In the New Testament it is quite clear that all the various ministerial functions (I Cor. 12:28 & Eph. 4:7-12 *cf.* Rom. 12:5-8) by which the life of the church is maintained and extended are 'gifts' (in Greek *charismata* = 'grace-gifts') of Christ to the church through the presence and operation of the Holy Spirit within it. Pastoral care is an important aspect of *Ministry* (Jn. 21:15 *ff*; I Pet. 5:2).

Subsequently, *Christian Ministry* within the church – which is the body of Christ empowered by the Holy Spirit – produces different members with a variety of gifts to sustain and enrich its life. This also makes it clear that all those who claim to be the followers of Jesus Christ are the members of *Christian Fellowship* and without any exception are called to *'Ministry'*.

72

VI. Christian Witness

Lesson 16

Go Forth into the World
Christian Home

In the last *Lesson*, we concluded with this remark that, 'all those who claim to be the *followers* of Jesus Christ are the members of the *Christian Fellowship* and without any exception are called to '*Ministry*''. This simply means that every Christian is not expected to be directly engaged in church work, while every Christian is called to be a *witness* to Jesus Christ. Before He was taken up Jesus said to the apostles whom He had chosen, '*you shall be my witnesses . . . to the end of the earth*' (Acts 1:8 RSV). As a result the church is a '*Witnessing Community*' and generation after generation, the same mandate has been handed over to the 'Witnessing Community'. The same has been passed on to us today to be His *witnesses* in this world within the context of life at home, community and the country.

At the end of the Confirmation Service, the Bishop gives the blessing starting with these words: '*Go forth into the world . . .* '

Question: What does it imply '*going into the world*'?

Explanation: The Holy Bible opens with a narration that after God had accomplished the Creation and development in preparation for man – that is, male and female (Gen.1:27); God '*planted a garden*' (Gen. 2:8), a '*home*' for them. Thus, after the creation of the universe the first institution was the '*home*' and not the church. It is *'home'* from where we first step out into the world.

It is rightly said that, 'a house is built with bricks and mortar; but, a *home* is made of human beings – initially husband and wife – which help to practice *'togetherness'* physically and with a sense of *'interdependency'* on each other emotionally and to be the sole masters of their married life. Ultimately, it constitutes human families which generally include father, mother, brothers and sisters including children.

Question: What is a *Christian Home*?

Explanation: First of all, we Christians too are part of a *Home*. A *Christian Home* is like any other *home* and also has been facing the same challenges of globalisation and the fast changing world. These changes have not spared even our rural societies where most of India still lives. The worst is that our youth also have been passing through stress and strain due to the impact of these changes.

Question: What are some of these challenges which we have been facing along with others?

Explanation: The United Nations Organisation (UNO) had declared 1994 as the *International Year of the Family*. Some of the problems that the family life has been experiencing are: Families battling with or already ruined by alcohol, drugs and gambling; fast marriages followed by fast divorces; extra-marital relationships; pre-marital sex followed by pre-marital pregnancies; parents who have to stay habitually away from home owing to employment elsewhere; families where money is the sole criterion; and families facing unemployment;

Broken families where the children become the main victims; Inter-faith marriages and ageing parents. The relationship between the parents and children is the root of our family life (Ex. 20:12). Above all, the demand of the modern life-style makes mostly the teenaged and youth of today unable to handle failure or adversity resulting in depression and even suicide.

Question: Are family problems cited above due to a lack of a sense of responsibility on the part of parents or the church or because of prevailing scenario in the world?

Explanation: May be all the three factors are responsible. When a *home* does not offer an atmosphere of one's own which helps every member of the *family* practice *'togetherness'* physically and lack a sense of *'interdependency'* emotionally, things are bound to go wrong.

Every *family* should at least have one meal a day *together* as it has emotional as well as social dimensions, preferably dinner. In the Book of Revelation to Saint John, Jesus says, *"Behold, I stand at the door and knock; if any one hears my voice and opens the door, I will come in to him and eat with him, and he with me"* (Rev. 3:20 RSV). A meal therefore has a religious significance. But a meal together at the end of the day should be without telephones or T.V., and be free from any problems. In fact, this occasion must be treated as *sacred* because it is here that the whole family *together* is enjoying God's provision for their physical sustenance. Sharing a meal time must be in an atmosphere of *thankfulness*. It is also an occasion to enjoy the fruit of one's own labour.

There are many things which children learn and inherit from their parents. It is often said that, *'the family that prays together, stays together'*. The discipline of *Family Prayer* is something precious which the parents can pass on to their children as a heritage. *Family Prayer* time must be observed with reverence (*shradha*), devotion (*bhakti*) and sincerity and not just as a routine in haste. Any house without earnest *Family Prayer* loses much of the blessing of a true Christian family. When we come to know daily of the conditions prevailing through T.V., Newspapers, etc., it seems that the world needs much more *Family Prayer* than ever before (Gen. 35:2-3). With all the scientific and technological advancements, the modern society we are living in is an era of social disintegration. *Love is what life is all about and we need to proclaim that 'God is Love'.*

Lesson 17

Go Forth into the World
Christian Life and the Neighbour

Indian *context* is 'religiously pluralistic' and 'culturally diverse'. We Christians as members of the *'Witnessing Community'* wherever we are – the place we live in, study or work, in market, bus or train or plane– we are always are in contact with those who are not Christians. We are in a minority and live in the midst of our *neighbours* who are both, *religiously* and to some extent *culturally* different from us. Because of the electronic media and mass communication as well as globalization the world is rapidly changing. The speed of travel has made us feel closer to one another as though we are all in one vast neighbourhood, which ultimately embraces the whole humanity. It is in such a *context* the following words of the Bishop, God *sends* out the newly confirmed:

'*Go forth into the world* in peace; be of good courage; hold fast that which is good; render to no one evil for evil; strengthen the fainthearted; support the weak; help the afflicted; honour every one; love and serve the Lord, rejoicing in the power of the Holy Spirit'.

Question: What does it mean to be 'Religiously Pluralistic' and 'Culturally Diverse'?

Explanation: Probably India is one country that gave birth to four major religions of the world – e.g., Hinduism, Buddhism,

Jainism and Sikhism – and four other major religions – e.g., Judaism, Christianity, Islam and Zoroastrianism – came to India and made it their home. Besides, there are also tribal religions. As a result, we Indians follow different religious faiths. This is what it is meant by the term *'Religiously Pluralistic'*.

As far as *'Cultural Diversity'* is concerned, to a greater extent, in our habits, emotions, feelings, music, dance, arts, etc., most of us have likings that are common. But, there are many more areas where we differ from one another. There are differences in life-style of those living in villages and those in the cities; those in the north and those in the south; there are differences between tribal and non-tribal and there are differences between the tribals of North-East India and those in Jharkhand, Orissa, Madhya Pradesh, etc.; and as a result, there are differences between the people belonging to different religious faiths and ideologies.

Question: In such a *'Religiously Pluralistic'* and *'Culturally Diverse'* context what should be the nature of *Christian Witness* to be more effective?

Explanation: Unfortunately, the church is an heavily institutionalized organization which is *alien* to the Indian *context* that is mainly influenced by Hinduism. Thus, what is needed is that the *Christian Witness* has to be communicated actively through Indian cultural ethos.

Question: How should the *Christian Witness* be made effective among the people of other faiths?

Explanation: Jesus said, "*You shall love your* neighbour *as yourself*" (Mt. 23:39 *cf.* Gal. 5:14 RSV). What is *'love'* is supposed to be? St. Paul defines the concept of *'love'* in his 'Love Song' written in his first letter to the Corinthians (I Cor. 13:13). In other words, we prove our love for God by loving our neighbour – anyone who is next to us or near us– though, it is not easy. But, this is how our Lord expects the *Christian Witness* to act in the *context* wherever we live and move.

Jesus further said, *'You know that the rulers of the Gentiles lord it over them, and their great men exercise authority over them. It shall not be so among you; but whoever would be great among you must be your slave; even as the Son of man came not to be served but to serve, and to give his life as a ransom for many'* (Mt. 20:25-28 RSV). Thus, the church – the *'Witnessing Community'* – is called to be a *Serving Community* (Mt. 25:31-46 *cf.* vs. 40).

People of other faiths are our spiritual *neighbours*. They are also, in the journey of life. They are in search for spiritual 'light' and 'truth'. Jesus said, *'I am the LIGHT of the world'* (Jn. 8:12 RSV) and *'I am ... the TRUTH ...'* (Jn. 14:6 RSV). On our part, we need to interpret the second Great Commandment in our attitude towards them. Jesus also said, *'Let your light so shine before men (and women) that they may see your good works and give glory to your Father who is in heaven'* (Mt. 5:16 RSV). The church as the Body of Christ – the *'Witnessing Community'* – is called to be present in the world as a sign of LOVE.

Lesson 18

Go Forth into the World
Christian Participation in Nation Building

Witness means to bear testimony to that which has happened. After His resurrection, the risen Lord charged His disciples, '*You shall be my witnesses . . . to the end of the earth*' (Acts 1:8 RSV). Consequently, through them the church has been commissioned. Thus, *witnessing* to the faith is in some sense a peculiar characteristic of Christian belief. For no one can genuinely claim to be a Christian believer unless he or she bears a living testimony to the redemptive work of God in Christ Jesus as a present reality.

In the previous *Lesson,* we reflected upon the fact that we – the '*Witnessing Community*' – are *called* to live in a *context* which is very much *religiously Pluralistic* and *Culturally Diverse*. Nevertheless Jesus said, '*As the Father has sent me, even so I send you*' (Jn. 20:21 RSV).

Question: How would this saying of Jesus be relevant in the *Indian context*?

Explanation: As Christians we are not *called* out of the world's *context* but into it. We are *Indians* not by our own choice, but because of our birth in this country by the will of God we have become *bon'a fid'e Indian* citizens. In the Gospel according to Saint John we read, '*There was a man sent from God, whose name was John. He came for testimony, to bear witness to the light, that all might believe through him'* (Jn. 1:6-7 RSV). These two verses teach us three important truths: First, the *source and origin of life*; secondly, the *purpose of life*; and, lastly, the *glory of life*. In other words, I am a man or a woman sent from God. As a result, the origin of my life is divine. Each one of us is sent that we may bear witness to the Light. It is a glorious thing if other people also become the *followers* of Jesus Christ because of the way we live our life.

God has a purpose for our life to be fulfilled here. Under the providence of God, we the *followers of Jesus Christ* are an integral part of *Indian* society and are *called upon* to proclaim Christ's power to reconcile and transform. We, like any other citizen of this Secular State are *called* to consider our role and play our part in the *Building of the Nation*. In accomplishing this and to play our part, we have to be *Christ-like* – '*As the Father has sent me, even so I send you*'.

Question: Being Christians as Indian citizens how can we make our contribution to the *Building of the Nation*?

Explanation: Constitutionally, India is a democratic country where all citizens have equal political rights. However, unless people at heart are converted to the democratic view of life they cannot realize the common good through democratic political institutions. There has to be a sense of social responsibility, economic justice, true community and sincere desire to adhere to democratic values. Hence we, the *followers* of Jesus Christ, have a special responsibility, not only to help the democratic structure of the government to work effectively, but also to translate the democratic values of life in terms of social action. Jesus said, *'Render to Caesar the things that are Caesar's, and to God the things that are God's'* (Mk. 12:17 cf. I Pet. 2:11-16 RSV).

Question: How do we translate the democratic values of life in terms of social action?

Explanation: Let us not be merely content with evangelistic programmes – such as: Evangelistic Campaigns, Tracts

Distribution, Conventions and Revival Meetings. The church – the *'Witnessing Community'* – is expected to be an instrument of God's redemptive action in Christ Jesus in the world today.

Saint Peter wrote two letters addressed to those Christians, who because of persecution, were scattered in different parts of Asia. The first thing that he reminds them is that the people of God are in the world, but not of it. Therefore, they are not to focus their goals and values on that which is transitory. (I Pet. 2:11-12). Secondly, Saint Peter focuses on *'submission'* of Christian citizens in relation to government authorities and all superiors (vss. 13-17).

Question: What is required of the church – the *'Witnessing Community'* – to accomplish its mission in the *Indian context*?

Explanation: We *Indian Christians* – especially those in big cities – seem to be more content to remain silent and anonymous, live by ourselves and for ourselves. By and large we are not concerned with the social issues taking place in our society, whereas we need to take to heart more seriously our Christian responsibility for the social changes that are overtaking our nation. *How?*

First and foremost fact is that we – the *'Witnessing Community'* – need to identify ourselves with current concerns of our secular life. We are called to live *with* our fellow *Indian* brothers and sisters, and yet be different *from* them. If God had to *incarnate* Himself – *'the Word became flesh and dwelt among us'* (Jn. 1:14a RSV) – then, why not the church – the 'Witnessing Community' – also truly become indigenous, think, speak and behave like those whom it addresses. For only then the *witnesses* become intelligibly effective and relevant to the common people of our great country.

PART TWO
Believers' Baptism

Lesson 1

Baptism in the New Testament
Jewish Proselyte Baptism

Every organization or association has some system by which a person can become a member. However, because of their respective nature and function, each system often varies with every organization and association. Generally, such systems require payment of monthly or annual or life 'Membership Fee'; expects certain rules and regulations to be followed; and, in some cases, one has even to go through publicly some kind of act either by making a promise(s) or signing a declaration of intention or making some offering and so on.

According to several religious systems, to get *initiated* as their members, one has to go through such acts or rituals.

The word *baptism* is derived from the Greek word *baptizein*, which simply means 'to dip into water to be cleansed from any kind of defilement'. The ceremonial washing as a part of preparation to approach God in prayer and worship is a common feature of several religions – such as Hinduism, Judaism (Lev. 8:6 & 14:9), Sikhism and Islam. Every year thousands of Hindus make journeys to have a dip in river Ganges or Yamuna or any other river that 'flow through our land bringing life, prosperity and cleansing to millions of people with a stirring in their souls a longing for release from their sins and union with God'.[33] Water is therefore a natural symbol for purification. In other words, the natural symbolism of 'water' is that it cleanses, refreshes and gives life and can be a sign of our life in God. It conveys a deep spiritual meaning.[34]

As we go through the pages of the Old Testament, we find 'water' appearing with great significance in many passages (Gen. 7:17-8:5; Ex. 14:19-31 & II Kgs. 5:1-15a). So much so, we find the use of 'water' among the Jews for purificatory purposes. As a matter of fact, by the time of our Lord the custom had been developed for proselytes to the Jewish faith to be not only circumcised but *baptized* also. These proselytes were known to be 'born again'. This was a new Jewish term for a proselyte; by immersing beneath the 'water' in *baptism* that represented a death to the old life and rising from the 'water', a birth to the new life within God's Covenant.

---

[33] Bishop Christopher Robinson, *Christian Initiation: Thanksgiving of Parents after the Birth of a Child, Blessing of Children & Receiving a Catechumen* (New Series No. 6), Delhi: ISPCK, May, 1987, p.4.

[34] Bishop Christopher Robinson, *Liturgical and Pastoral Notes: Believers' Baptism* (New Series No. 7), Delhi: ISPCK, May 1987, p. 5.

Lesson 2

Baptism in the New Testament
Baptism by John the Baptist

In the last *Lesson*, we saw that by the time of our Lord the custom had already arisen for proselytes to the Jewish faith to be not only circumcised but also *baptized*.

Interestingly, when we go through the pages of the four Gospels we come across references about John the Baptist and his work. In the New Testament, John is also called *'the Baptizer'* (Mk. 1:4; 6:14 & 24) and *'the Baptist'* (Mk. 6:25; 8:28; Mt. 3:1; 11:11 & 12;14:2 & 8; 16:14; 17:13; Lk. 7:20 & 33; 9:19).

We read in the Gospel according to Saint Mark that, 'John the *Baptizer* appeared in the wilderness preaching a *baptism* of repentance for the forgiveness of sins' (Mk. 1:5 RSV); and that there was discussion about him between Jesus and the Pharisees (Mk. 11:30). His *baptism* is presented as a symbolic washing in the river Jordan but with repentance. He, of course, was the agent. His *baptism* was also known in other places such as Alexandria (Acts 18:25 & 19:1-7).

The *baptism* of John differed from the ordinary ceremonial washings of the Jews because it was not repeated. It was preparatory for the coming of the Messianic Kingdom (Mt. 3:2).

John's *baptism* was only a *'water-baptism unto repen*tance'. He himself looked forward to the coming of the One who would bestow not only forgiveness from the past, but grant new power for the future (Mt. 3:11b; Mk. 1:8).

Lesson 3

Baptism in the New Testament
As Received by Our Lord Himself

As we have noted earlier, the practice of *baptism* was already familiar to the Jews and easily understood by those who were not Jews.

Since Jesus was sinless (Heb. 4:15); the pertinent question that needs to be looked into is as to why then was He *baptized* by John (Mk. 1:9)? There may be at least four reasons: (i) to connect Himself with John the prophet who prepared the way for the Messiah; (ii) to identify Himself with the sinful race He came to redeem (Mt. 3:16-17); (iii) to establish the course of His own ministry; and (iv) to inaugurate that ministry officially. Moreover, the fact that Jesus Himself submitted to John's baptism shows that there was a link, if not a recognizable continuity between His movement and John's.

✡ ✡ ✡ ✡ ✡ ✡ ✡

Let us have a quick look at the *baptism* during the Apostolic Age – that is, the period following the Ascension of our Lord. At Pentecost, Peter calls on all to '*repent and be baptized*' in order to receive the promised gift of the Spirit (Acts 2:38). It means: '(a) a sign of cleansing from sins; (b) of engrafting into Christ; (c) of entrance into the Covenant of grace; and (d) to have fellowship with Christ in His death and resurrection and of rising to newness of life'.[35]

For Paul it was baptism 'into Christ' – that is, into union with Him, to be possessed by Him, to receive all benefits (Gal. 3:27; I Cor. 1:13 &12:13; Rom. 6:4). Although, the 'water' in *baptism* certainly symbolizes the washing away of sin, it almost means 'to wash oneself'. 'Moreover, it also links us first to the whole experience of the Exodus of Israelites through the Red Sea (Ex. 13:17-4:31), that is, from slavery in Egypt to freedom in the Promised Land'; this was an experience of going 'from death to life' (*Ref.* Ex. 14:13-14).

This establishes the fact that from the Apostolic Age, *baptism* had become universal as the means of *entry* into the church and an *initiatory* rite and a *sacrament* of the Christian Church. The word '*sacrament*' in Latin means 'a sacred pledge'. The term however, is limited to those rites which were commanded in the New Testament and ordained by Christ our Lord in the Gospels – *Baptism* and *the Supper of the Lord*. A *sacrament* is defined as 'an outward and visible sign of an inward and spiritual gift of God' – that is, '*grace*'.

✿ ✿ ✿ ✿ ✿ ✿ ✿

Although, in the beginning the Jews who became Christians continued going to the Temple of Jerusalem to pray (Acts 3:1); the centre of their worship was the '*Breaking of the Bread*' (Acts 2:42 & 46). Soon after Pentecost, the early church changed the weekly day of Worship from Saturday (the Sabbath for the Jews) to Sunday. Because, it was on the Feast of the Passover Jesus died. On this feast the Jews celebrated their deliverance from the slavery of Pharaoh in Egypt. The Christians understood that the deliverance of the Jews from Egypt

---

[35] *The Constitution of the Church of North India and Bye-Laws* (as amended up to 21st October, 2005), Part I, Chapter I, Section V, Sub-Section A, Clause 2, Delhi: ISPCK, 2006, p. 16.

through Moses was *only a symbol* of their deliverance through the death and resurrection of Jesus Christ, from the slavery of the devil at *Baptism*. The early Christians, therefore chose the date of the Jewish Passover to celebrate the passing from *the death of sin into a new life with Christ*. Although they kept the name of the feast to be the same, for them it had a far deeper meaning than it had for the Jews as it was their true *Easter*. Later on, in English, the term Feast of Passover took the name of *Easter*.

'The Feast of Incarnation of our Lord' – that is: *Christmas* – is not the oldest feast of the church. It was only about 330 years after the birth of Jesus Christ that Christians in Rome started celebrating it on December 25. Since the very early years, the church celebrated only one feast, that of *Easter* – 'The Feast of the Resurrection of our Lord' – It was celebrated every Sunday – the Lord's Day (Acts 20:7 & Rev. 1:10) – and was regarded as a *small feast of Easter*.

During the passage of time certain developments took place. In the beginning, Christians celebrated both the *Death* and *Resurrection of Jesus* together during Friday, Saturday and Sunday – '*The Holy Three Days*' as they were called since ancient days. Then, this was extended to the *whole week* starting from the previous Sunday. Thus, the *Holy Week,* came into being as we call it now.

One of the significant events that used to take place on Easter barring an emergency, the *baptisms* were mainly administered on this day, though *baptisms* were not easily granted. Since persecution was common in those days *baptism* was administered to only those who offered sufficient guarantee of perseverance. The candidates – '*catechumen*' preparing for *baptism* – had to go through an intensive course of instruction in the Faith, which lasted for several years. Besides, during Lenten period *a final stage of preparation lasting three weeks* before Easter was established.

In the very early days of the church, the mission was mainly directed towards adults.[36] Thus, the process was one single rite – that is the *Baptism*, with the *Gift of the Holy Spirit* followed by the first *Communion*. During the course of time because of practical contemporary needs this practice has changed.

---

[36]Bishop Christopher Robinson, *Liturgical and Pastoral Notes: Christian Initiation, Thanksgiving of Parents after the Birth of a Child, Blessing of Children, Receiving a Catechumen* (New Series No. 6), Delhi: ISPCK, May 1987, p. 2.

APPENDIX

The House of Worship of the Lord

'The Lord appeared to Solomon a second time, and said to him, "I have heard your prayer and your supplication, which you have made before me; I have consecrated this house which you have built, and put my name there for ever; my eyes and my heart will be there for all time"' (I Kgs. 9:2-3 RSV).

Over forty years ago, the evening before I was to write my paper on Worship; I went to my college (Bishop's College, Kolkata) library to find some material just to substantiate my knowledge on the subject. I picked up a book on Worship – a paperback edition of about two hundred pages written by a *Baptist Pastor* in England – from the shelf, exclusively for the New Arrival. I went back to my room and skipped through the book. I must say I have not read such an interesting book on Worship with simple and practical information. Since I was under the pressure of the examination next morning, I forgot to note down the name of the author and publisher. Even today, I regret this lapse.

Since it is a long time I read the book, I do not remember the exact words. The writer began something like this: 'The church building and everything in it must be a help in our worship. They must be means to uplift us spiritually but not be an end in itself. We must know why they are there and what is their purpose? Each item must have its proper place in the church. So, whatever we do as a part of our worship we must do with an understanding and reverence and with a sense of offering to God'.

I. CHURCH BUILDINGS

Through Gospel accounts we come to know that according to Jewish tradition Jesus used to go to the Temple (Mk. 12:35, Lk. 2:46, Jn. 2:14 & 7:14) and the synagogue (Mk. 3:2 & Lk. 4:16) on the Sabbath day. We also find that most of the time Jesus used to retire to a lonely place (Mt. 26:36, Mk. 9:2, Lk. 4:2 & 6:12) in silence for prayer. Jesus had His last supper with His disciples in the Upper Room (Lk. 22:12). After His ascension for sometime the disciples continued worshipping in the temple (Acts 2:46 & 3:1) and the synagogue (Acts 18:4), but breaking bread was in their homes (Acts 2:46).

Today, we see different architectural forms of church buildings, both simple and elaborate, small and big. These different types of church buildings tell us two things: first, of the historical era and the thinking of the church of that time; and secondly, the tradition of the church which worships in a particular building. Church buildings belonging to Roman Catholic, former Anglican or Orthodox traditions, all of episcopal background are usually elaborate. Those of the reformed traditions, are simple. Many of the churches of the Church of the North India are of this tradition.

The church buildings of those having ancient episcopal tradition can be divided into various sections. For example, in several churches (with special reference to Anglican tradition) as we enter through the main door (not from the side doors) there is a place for *enquirers* or *catechumen*. Since they are not baptized and are not yet real members of God's family, they are treated just like friends of the family. In olden days, they were made to sit here only. Further in, is the *Baptismal Font* which signifies that it is through baptism that we enter God's family, the church. Thirdly, is the place where the faithful sit for Worship. This large area is known as *'Nave'* which means 'ship', as, this is one of the symbols that is used for the church – that carries God's people across the sea of life. Fourthly the *'Chancel'*, usually a raised up space where on the left hand side is the 'Pulpit', an elevated erection from where Christ crucified is proclaimed and on the right hand is the 'Lectern'. The word 'Lesson' is derived from it. It is a stand to keep the Holy Bible for reading the Lessons during the Service. The clergy and choir also sit in the *Chancel*. Fifthly, *Altar Rails* where the worshippers kneel to receive Holy Communion. Sixthly, is the area which is commonly known as *Sanctuary*. On one side of it is placed Bishop's Chair and on the other side (Right-hand) Credence Table to keep Chalice, Paten, Bread, Wine, Water, etc. Seventhly, there is *'Altar'* or *'Communion Table'*. Normally, on the 'Altar' there is an empty 'Cross' symbolizing the Resurrection of Jesus. There are candlesticks also on the Altar showing 'Jesus is the Light of the World and the glory of His people'. Lastly, is the side *Chapel(s)*. It is normally dedicated to the Virgin Mary and hence is called 'Lady Chapel'. If there is another Chapel, dedicated to some other saint it will be named as St. Thomas' Chapel. These are used for week-day services.

In some CNI churches for the believers' baptism, the baptism is held by immersion, either in a pond or a river or in a baptismal pool outside the church building or inside it.

II. VESTMENTS (DRESS OF THE CLERGY)

The use of the *vestments* in the church was introduced several centuries ago with two basic purposes: for *simplicity* and *uniformity* among the clergy. In the Church of North India, for the ordained ministers the *cassock* with *girdle* is recommended. It is a long white gown which once used to be the daily dress of the clergy both indoors and outdoors. While conducting the Worship he/she is expected to put on the *surplice* of white linen reaching upto the knees. Over which it is also expected to put on the CNI *red stole*.

III. SACRAMENT VESSELS

Normally, Chalice, Paten or set of small individual cups are used for serving the *Holy Communion*. Besides, cruets for wine and water and a box for wafers or bread are required.

IV. CHURCH'S YEAR & LITURGICAL COLOURS

The Seasons of the Christian Year follows the life of Jesus which helps us in remembering the great truths of the Christian Faith based on certain events that have happened once for all, bring to our memories year after year. They are the *Birth of Jesus*, His *'Going to the Father'* – that is: His Crucifixion, Resurrection and Ascension – and *His gift of the Holy Spirit*.

The year begins with *Advent,* which means coming. The church prepares and gets ready for the birth of Jesus called *Christmas*, the 'Feast of the Incarnation of our Lord'. This is followed by the *Feast of Epiphany*, manifestation of Jesus as Divine when the Three Wise Men came from the East to worship Him. When Jesus was grown up, He spent forty days in the wilderness in preparation for His ministry. The church observes this period as *Lent* that starts with *Ash Wednesday*. The last days of our Lord's ministry are observed as the *Holy Week or Passion Week*, which ends on *Good Friday* when He was crucified. Death and burial were not the end for Jesus, nor will they be for us. They usher in a new beginning. Jesus rose from the grave on *Easter Day* to live forever. That is why every Sunday, the day He rose is a joyful memorial of His resurrection. For the next forty days Jesus kept on appearing to His disciples. Then on the *Ascension Day*, He returned to reign in heaven. But the disciples, like us needed strength. Jesus had promised that He would not leave them 'comfortless' (i.e. strengthless) – '*I will not leave you desolate; I will come to you*' (Jn. 14:18 RSV). He came as the Holy Spirit at *Pentecost*, commonly known as Whitsunday. This brings us almost to half of the year. The rest of the half year, normally spans for a period of twenty-five to twenty-eight Sundays. During this period we ponder upon the wonderful things that Jesus taught and did.

In some churches, these Seasons and the Feasts are marked by distinctive colours. The vestments or stole worn at Holy Communion, the altar frontal, the markers in the Holy Bible on the lectern, the pulpit fall, the cloth which hangs from the pulpit book-rest, are changed accordingly. This helps us in remembering the systematic progress of the church's Year. *White or Gold* is for the joyful Festivals, especially Christmas, Epiphany, Easter and Ascension and also Saints' Days other than Martyrs. *Red* (stands for *fire* or *blood*): Whitsunday and commemoration of Martyrs. *Purple* (stands for *penitence* and *preparation*): Lent and Advent . Green (common colour for *Nature,* reminding us of *God's provision for our needs*): Sundays after Whitsunday and the Epiphany.

www.ingramcontent.com/pod-product-compliance
Lightning Source LLC
Chambersburg PA
CBHW032128090426
42743CB00007B/510